ONE POT FEEDS ALL

DARINA ALLEN

ONE POT FEEDS ALL

100 new recipes
from roasting tin dinners
to one-pan desserts

Photography by Lizzie Mayson

Kyle Books

An Hachette UK Company
www.hachette.co.uk

First published in Great Britain in 2019 by
Kyle Books, an imprint of Kyle Cathie Ltd
Carmelite House
50 Victoria Embankment
London EC4Y 0DZ
www.kylebooks.co.uk

ISBN: 978 0 857835 758, 978 0 857838 384

Text copyright 2019 © Darina Allen
Design and layout copyright 2019 © Kyle Cathie Ltd

Darina Allen is hereby identified as the author
of this work in accordance with Section 77 of the
Copyright, Designs and Patents Act 1988.

All rights reserved. No part of this work may be
reproduced or utilised in any form or by any
means, electronic or mechanical, including
photocopying, recording or by any information
storage and retrieval system, without the prior
written permission of the publisher.

A Cataloguing in Publication record for this title
is available from the British Library

Printed and bound in China

10 9 8 7 6 5 4 3 2

Dedication
For all the heroic young
couples who are trying to
keep all the balls in the air.

Publisher JOANNA COPESTICK
Editor VICKY ORCHARD
Editorial assistant SARAH KYLE
Design HELEN BRATBY
Photography LIZZIE MAYSON*
Food styling ANNIE RIGG
Props styling LINDA BERLIN
Production GEMMA JOHN

*Excludes portrait on page 6 © Peter Cassidy

Contents

INTRODUCTION

One pot, one dish, one roasting tin, I can't believe it's taken me so long to write this book as it's been bubbling away in my subconscious for years. It is over a decade since we added a One-Pot Wonders course to our schedule at the Ballymaloe Cookery School. From the word go it was a big hit and its enduring popularity is a sure sign that this way of cooking is here to stay.

This book is for all of you who really want to cook delicious, wholesome food for yourselves and those you love, but find it virtually impossible to keep all the balls in the air, battling home through rush hour traffic, dashing into the shops to grab some ingredients and then doing your best to cook from scratch, in full knowledge that beautiful freshly cooked produce has the best flavour and is super nutritious. For growing numbers of people, it's simply not possible – yet I can still hear my mother's words ringing in my ears, 'If you don't get wholesome, nourishing, delicious food onto the table to keep the family healthy, happy and bouncing with energy, you'll give the money to the doctor or the chemist'. But what to do?

Well, hopefully this book will provide some solutions. I've collected my favourite one-pot dishes, some time-honoured favourites honed over the years, others developed more recently when we were testing recipes specifically for this book. Because my brief was that everything had to be cooked in one pot, against my better judgement, I experimented with some one-pot pasta dishes with great success. By increasing the liquid in some other dishes, I discovered that I could add rice, pearl barley, orzo and beans to the various

pots with delicious results – so you really can get your whole meal from one dish. Of course, you can still cook them separately, if you like, but believe me this one-pot method works brilliantly.

It's not just pots and pans – my roasting tin and baking trays are in constant use. I love to layer up gratins and to roast fish and meat over vegetables, or just roast a selection of vegetables with lots of gutsy herbs and olive oil.

Some recipes, such as Lamb & Pearl Barley Stew (page 74), are naturally one-pot dishes, with chunks of sweet lamb, carrots, onions, a sprig of thyme. But there are plenty more examples.

Many of these one-pot recipes reheat brilliantly, or can be frozen in portions to make your life easier on another occasion, such as the Super-easy Chicken Casserole (page 57), Chilli con Carne (page 65), Cod, Hake or Haddock with Dill and Pangratatto (page 101), Venison & Parsnip Stew (page 85), Lamb, Butternut Squash & Orzo Stew (page 76) or the Black-eyed Bean, Pumpkin & Chickpea Stew (page 124).

So, what's not to love about one-pot, one-dish, or one-roasting-tin cooking? For a start, there's less washing up. It's a brilliant option if you don't have much time and there's no longer any need to feel guilt-ridden. With the recipes in this book, you simply pop everything into the pot, add some herbs and spices, bring to the boil, cover and put into the

oven or simmer on the hob while you catch up with other chores, help with homework or just put your feet up and enjoy a well-deserved cup of tea or glass of wine. This way of cooking is also perfect for easy entertaining – who doesn't love a juicy stew or casserole? Ladle it out at the table directly from the pot and follow it with a salad of organic leaves for a perfect meal.

An electric slow cooker or crockpot is also worth considering as part of your kitchen kit, perfect for slow cooking and gentle braises and of course for making stock.

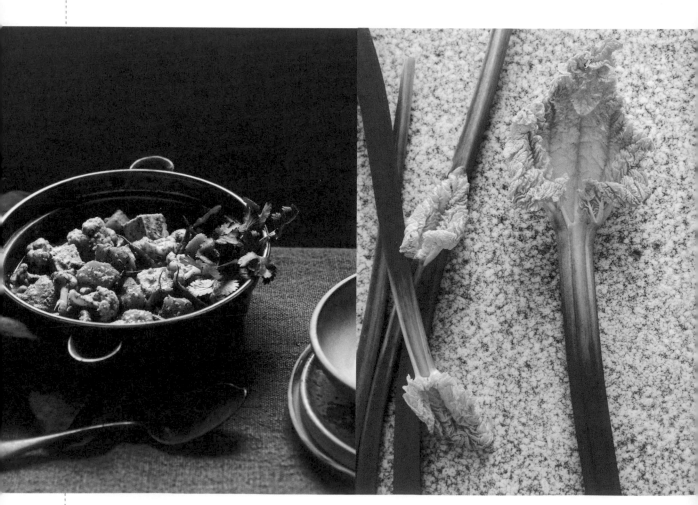

Pots, pans, tins & trays

You don't need much in the way of kitchen kit, but it's good to invest in a few sturdy pots and casseroles. Buy the best quality you can afford so they are durable and will last a lifetime. Seek out a heavy iron pot that can be used on the hob and also in the oven. If you buy just one piece of equipment, this is the one-pot essential to invest in.

I love my 29cm heavy, black Le Creuset pot with a tight-fitting lid. It's chic enough to bring to the table and large enough to make a stew or tagine to feed everyone for family supper or to share with friends for dinner. If you're cooking for smaller numbers, a 22cm round or 25cm oval enamel casserole is also a good investment.

A 1.2-litre Pyrex pie dish is perfect for sweet or savoury puddings, such as Indian Rice Pudding (page 191) and numerous savoury bread puddings such as Gruyère, Piquillo Pepper & Basil Bread & Butter Pudding (page 139)

Several heavy enamel baking trays with a lip, a good stainless steel roasting tin and a couple of gratin dishes, which could be Pyrex, pottery, earthenware or stainless steel, are perfect for the Soda Bread Pizza (page 160) or Toad in the Hole (page 83). Le Creuset also make a gratin dish (21 x 29cm) that I use again and again for dishes like Roast Scallops (page 97) or Roasted Peaches, Nectarines or Apricots with Honey & Lavender (page 184). I also love my lidded, heavy, stainless-steel Penthole sauté pans that can go on the hob and in the oven, as used in a number of recipes. I have two sizes: 22cm and 26cm. They even double up as cake tins.

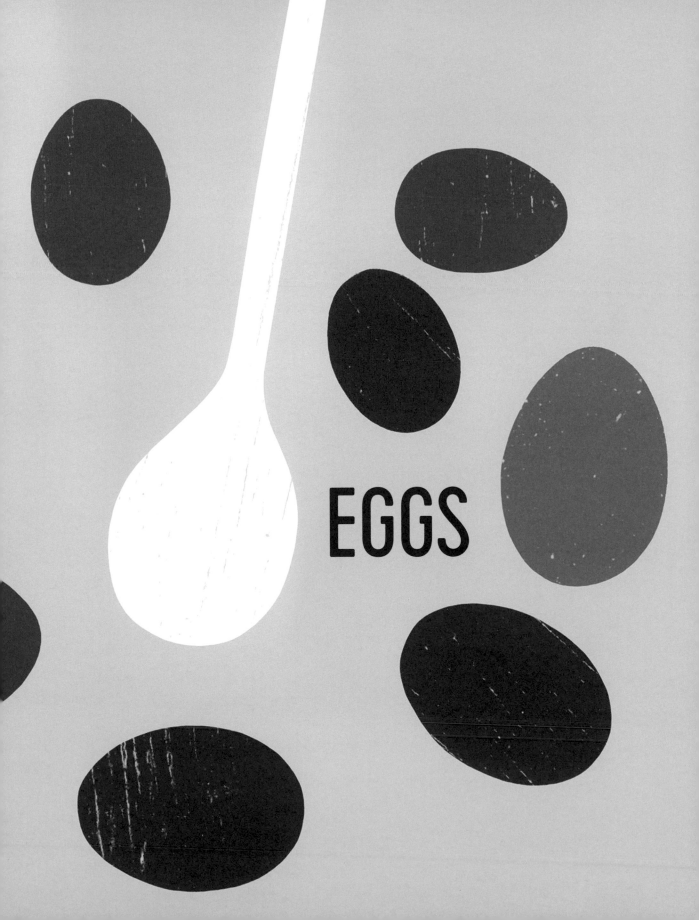

EGGS

There are so many variations on this much-loved Middle Eastern dish, which is also a favourite around the Mediterranean and Tunisia. This makes a fantastic Sunday brunch or supper dish.

Shakshuka

- ½–1 teaspoon caraway seeds
- 50ml extra virgin olive oil, plus extra to drizzle
- 1 medium onion, thinly sliced
- 1 red pepper, deseeded and thinly sliced
- 1 teaspoon chilli flakes
- 1 teaspoon ground cumin
- 1 teaspoon sweet smoked paprika, to taste
- 2 large ripe tomatoes, chopped
- 2 x 400g tins of plum tomatoes, chopped
- 8 organic, free-range eggs
- 50g feta cheese
- 2 tablespoons chopped coriander leaves
- flaky sea salt, freshly ground black pepper and a pinch of sugar
- sourdough bread, to serve

Preheat the oven to 200°C/gas mark 6.

Sprinkle the caraway seeds into a 25cm heavy, ovenproof frying pan and toast over a medium heat for 2–3 minutes until the seeds become a shade darker and smell fragrant. Add the extra virgin olive oil and continue to cook for a further minute or two. Reduce the heat.

Add the sliced onion and pepper and cook for 5–8 minutes until soft and jammy. Add the chilli flakes, cumin and paprika and cook for a further 3–4 minutes, stirring.

Stir in the chopped tomatoes and cook for 5 minutes before adding the tinned tomatoes and a pinch of sugar. Bring slowly to the boil and season with salt and pepper. Reduce the heat to low and simmer gently for 20–25 minutes until the sauce is thick, rich and delicious.

Take a wooden spoon and hollow out eight little 'wells' in the surface of the sauce for the eggs. Crack in the eggs and, taking care not to break the yolks, use a spoon to bury the egg whites gently under the sauce – leaving the yolks uncovered. Crumble the feta over the egg whites (not the yolks) and drizzle with extra virgin olive oil.

Transfer the pan to the oven and bake for 5 minutes for 'just set' yolks and 7–8 minutes for harder yolks.

Remove from the oven. Sprinkle with plenty of coriander, drizzle with extra virgin olive oil and season with a sprinkling of flaky sea salt.

Serve with lots of fresh or toasted sourdough for dipping.

A super 'master' recipe, also known as shirred eggs, or simply as baked eggs. Nothing could be simpler: take a few eggs and a few good things from your fridge or pantry, combine everything together and tuck in. There are infinite variations – just make sure your eggs are super-fresh and the cream is rich and unctuous.

Baked eggs *with smoked mackerel & dill*

- 15g butter
- 2 smoked mackerel fillets, broken into flakes
- 2 tablespoons chopped dill
- 6–8 tablespoons double cream
- 4 organic, free-range eggs
- flaky sea salt and freshly ground black pepper
- chopped flat-leaf parsley and pul biber
- crusty bread (optional), to serve

Lightly butter a 19cm round or oval gratin dish. Sprinkle the smoked mackerel and dill over the base. Pour half of the cream into the dish and carefully break in the eggs. Season with salt and pepper. Spoon the remaining cream over the top.

Place the dish in a bain-marie of hot water, cover with a lid and bring to a simmer on the hob. Continue to cook either gently on the hob or, uncovered, in a moderate oven at 180°C/ gas mark 4 for about 10 minutes for a soft egg, or 12 minutes for a firmer egg.

Serve immediately, sprinkled with chopped parsley and pul biber. Accompany with some crusty bread, if you wish.

Variations

CHEESY BAKED EGGS

Follow the recipe above, omitting the mackerel and dill. Top each egg with ½–1 tablespoon of finely grated Parmesan, Gruyère or Cheddar cheese (or a mixture) and bake, uncovered, in a bain-marie in the oven as in the recipe above.

BAKED EGGS WITH YOGURT & PAPRIKA OIL

Follow the recipe for Cheesy Baked Eggs, omitting the cheese. After the creamy eggs come out of the oven, top each one with a dollop of natural yogurt and drizzle with paprika oil (made by gently heating 1 teaspoon of sweet or smoked paprika with 4 tablespoons of extra virgin olive oil).

BAKED EGGS WITH
ANCHOVIES & PUL BIBER

Lightly butter a 19cm round or oval
gratin dish and add 4 tablespoons
of double cream. Crack in 4 eggs
and lay a beautiful anchovy on top
of each. Top each with another
spoonful of cream and sprinkle
with pul biber or, better still, a
mixture of pul biber and some
freshly roasted ground cumin.
Bake in a bain-marie in the oven,
as above, and serve scattered with
freshly chopped flat-leaf parsley.

OEUFS EN COCOTTE
WITH TOMATO FONDUE

Lightly butter a 19cm round or oval
gratin dish and put 4 tablespoons
of Tomato Fondue (page 133)
in the bottom. Top with 4 eggs
and spoon over 4 tablespoons of
double cream. Season with salt
and pepper and top each egg with
½–1 tablespoon of finely grated
cheese. If you wish, include a
little cooked bacon or some diced
chorizo. Bake, uncovered, in a
bain-marie in the oven as above.

This riff on the classic French omelette is one of my favourites. I've added some spices, but you can have fun dreaming up your own flavours and additions. The quintessential fast food, this Masala omelette is tender and delicious – and oozing with flavour.

Masala omelette

- 1 ripe tomato, finely chopped
- ¼ teaspoon green chilli, finely chopped
- 1 tablespoon chopped coriander
  (leaves and stalks), plus extra to garnish
- 2 organic, free-range eggs
- 2 teaspoons whole milk or water
- ¼ teaspoon ground cumin
- ¼ teaspoon ground coriander
- a pinch of ground turmeric
- 1 tablespoon chopped spring onion
- 2 teaspoons extra virgin olive oil or
  clarified butter (see below)
- hot sauce (optional), to serve
- flaky sea salt, freshly ground black
  pepper and a pinch of sugar

CLARIFIED BUTTER

Melt 225g butter gently in a saucepan or in a Pyrex jug in a low oven at 150°C/ gas mark 2. Leave it to stand for a few minutes, then spoon the crusty white layer of salt particles off the top of the melted butter. Underneath this crust there is clear liquid butter, which is called clarified butter. The milky liquid at the bottom can be discarded or used in a white sauce. Clarified butter is excellent for cooking because it can withstand a higher temperature when the salt and milk solids are removed. It will keep, covered, in the fridge for several weeks.

Warm a serving plate in the oven. Season the chopped tomato with salt, pepper and sugar.

Preheat a 23cm non-stick omelette pan over the highest heat. Have the tomato and chilli ready beside you on the hob, along with a spoon and a plastic spatula and the chopped coriander.

Whisk the eggs, milk or water and spices, spring onion and chilli in a bowl until thoroughly combined, but not too fluffy. Season with salt and pepper. Put the warmed plate beside the hob because you won't have time to go looking for it later.

Add the clarified butter or olive oil to the pan. As soon as it sizzles, pour in the egg mixture. It will start to cook immediately, so quickly pull the edges of the omelette towards the centre with a plastic spatula, tilting the pan backwards and forwards, then up and down for another few seconds so that the uncooked egg runs to the sides. Continue right around the pan until most of the egg is set and it will not run easily any more. The centre should still be soft and moist – don't worry, it will be perfectly set by the time it gets to the table. Sprinkle the seasoned tomato, chilli and chopped coriander over the surface of the omelette.

To fold the omelette, use the spatula to flip the omelette edge nearest the handle of the pan over the filling, towards the centre. Then change your grip of the handle so you are holding it from underneath; this will make it more comfortable for you to hold as you tilt it upright. Tilt the pan so it is almost upright and, hey presto, the top of omelette will roll towards the bottom of the pan.

Half-roll and half-slide the omelette onto the plate so that it lands folded into three. Garnish with a couple of sprigs of coriander. Serve immediately with a salad of organic leaves, some good bread, a glass of wine and maybe a dash of hot sauce, if you wish.

A cross between a pancake and an omelette, these roll-ups are fast and fun to make with family and friends.

Variations

SMOKED MACKEREL, DILLISK & CHIVES

Omit the ground spices, spring onion and chilli and replace with 2 tablespoons of smoked mackerel flakes, a generous sprinkle of dried dillisk and freshly chopped chives. Sprinkle the flaked mackerel, dillisk and chopped chives on the omelette just before folding. Save a little extra for garnish.

TOMATO FONDUE & BOCCONCINI – WITH OR WITHOUT PESTO

Omit the ground spices, spring onion and chilli and replace with 2 tablespoons of hot Tomato Fondue (page 133) and 4–5 bocconcini. Add the tomato fondue and bocconcini, fold. Sprinkle over some basil and flat-leaf parsley leaves to garnish.

A LITTLE 'NDUJA & FLAT-LEAF PARSLEY

Omit the ground spices, spring onion and chilli and replace with a filling of 25g diced 'nduja and 1 tablespoon of chopped flat-leaf parsley. Fold and garnish with extra chopped parsley.

TANSY

Adding tansy to the eggs is a revelation. Follow the main recipe, omitting the ground spices, spring onion and chilli and replacing them with 1 teaspoon of chopped tansy added to the egg mixture.

Omelette *roll-ups*

- 4 organic, free-range eggs
- 2 tablespoons water or whole milk
- 2 tablespoons extra virgin olive oil or clarified butter (page 16)
- flaky sea salt and freshly ground black pepper
- rocket leaves, to serve

FOR THE FILLING

- a small handful of organic salad leaves per person
- ½ cucumber, peeled and cut into long sticks
- 2–3 tablespoons sliced spring onions
- 1–2 avocados, peeled, stoned and sliced
- 3–4 tomatoes, sliced and seasoned with salt, pepper and a sprinkling of sugar
- tomato relish, to serve (optional)

Whisk together the eggs and milk or water in a bowl. Season with salt and pepper.

Preheat a 25cm non-stick pan over the highest heat and add a dash of extra virgin olive oil or clarified butter. Pour enough of the egg mixture into the pan to coat the base evenly – it should sizzle and set almost immediately. Flip the omelette over and cook the other side for a few seconds, then slide it out of the pan onto a plate.

Repeat the process until all of the omelette mixture is used up, stacking the omelettes on top of one another.

Fill the omelettes with the fillings of your choice, then roll them up and serve on a bed of rocket leaves.

This was a favourite Allen family supper dish when I first came to Ballymaloe in the late 1960s. It was simply called Flat Omelette... but after a Danish intern told us it was exactly like the omelette her family enjoyed on Funen, it was renamed Danish Omelette and so it has been ever since.

Danish family omelette

- 8 large organic, free-range eggs
- 25ml water
- 25g butter
- 4 tablespoons diced cooked ham, bacon, chorizo or merguez
- 1 generous tablespoon freshly chopped flat-leaf parsley
- 1 tablespoon freshly chopped chives
- flaky sea salt and freshly ground black pepper
- tomato salad and green salad leaves, to serve

Crack the eggs into a large bowl, add the water and season generously with salt and pepper. Whisk vigorously until the mixture fluffs up and increases in volume by three or four times.

Melt the butter in a 25cm metal or non-stick frying pan over a medium heat. When it foams, swirl the butter around the sides of the pan. Pour in the egg mixture, reduce the heat and cook for 6–7 minutes until the bottom is set. Don't stir.

Sprinkle the cooked ham, bacon, chorizo or merguez over the top. It will sink through the frothy surface. Scatter with the freshly chopped herbs, but don't fold them in.

Serve immediately from the pan while still warm. I bring the pan to the table and serve the omelette in segments alongside a tomato salad and some organic leaves.

Good things to add to a frittata

ASPARAGUS, ROCKET & WILD GARLIC

Follow the main recipe, replacing the meat, goat's cheese and tomatoes with 150g blanched asparagus tips, a handful of rocket and 4 tablespoons of chopped wild garlic leaves.

PEA SHOOTS, PEAS & MINT

Follow the main recipe, replacing the meat, goat's cheese and tomatoes with 2 handfuls of pea shoots, 150g cooked peas and 1–2 tablespoons of chopped mint.

CHILLI & CORIANDER

Follow the main recipe, omitting the herbs and replacing the meat, goat's cheese and tomato with ½–1 diced red chilli and 1 tablespoon of freshly chopped coriander.

SMOKED SALMON & GOAT'S CHEESE

Follow the main recipe, replacing the meat and tomatoes with 110–175g diced smoked salmon. Replace the herbs with fresh dill.

WILD GARLIC

Follow the main recipe, replacing the meat, goat's cheese and tomatoes with 2 handfuls of chopped wild garlic leaves. Garnish with wild garlic flowers, if available.

ROAST PUMPKIN, GOAT'S CHEESE & ROCKET

Follow the main recipe, replacing the meat and tomatoes with 550g diced roasted pumpkin and 2 handfuls of rocket.

COURGETTE BLOSSOM & MINT

Follow the main recipe, replacing the meat, goat's cheese and tomatoes with 175g diced and sautéed courgettes, 1 cup of courgette blossoms, torn into pieces, and 1–2 tablespoons of chopped mint. Tarragon is delicious here also but use sparingly.

SERVES 6-8

Every teenager should be able to whip up a frittata before they leave school. It's a brilliant basic recipe to have in your repertoire, a one-pan dish that will feed family and friends. It can, of course, be super simple with just a few fresh herbs and cheese – or you could go all out with some delicious chunky morsels of smoked fish or spicy sausage, goat's cheese or bocconcini, cherry tomatoes and fresh basil leaves. Enjoy for breakfast, lunch, dinner or a picnic, or cut into cubes to serve with drinks. A frittata can be served directly from the pan for a rustic family meal. Frittata were originally cooked on the hob, but nowadays I prefer to bake mine gently in the oven.

Chorizo, goat's cheese & tomato frittata

- 10 large organic, free-range eggs
- 1 teaspoon flaky sea salt and lots of freshly ground black pepper
- 2 tablespoons chopped flat-leaf parsley
- 2 teaspoons thyme leaves
- 2 tablespoons freshly chopped basil or marjoram
- 75g Gruyère cheese, grated
- 25g Parmesan cheese, grated
- 110–175g chorizo, merguez or saucisses de Toulouse, cut into 1cm dice
- 450g cherry tomatoes, halved
- 25g butter
- 110g goat's cheese

TO SERVE
- rocket leaves
- extra virgin olive oil
- either a good green salad or a tomato and basil leaf salad

Crack the eggs into a bowl and whisk in the salt, freshly ground black pepper, fresh herbs and grated cheeses. Carefully fold in the chorizo and tomatoes.

Melt the butter in a 22.5cm non-stick frying pan and when it starts to foam, tip in the well-whisked eggs. Then arrange the goat's cheese in blobs evenly over the top.

THERE ARE TWO COOKING METHODS:
Either Reduce the heat as low as it will go and leave the eggs to cook gently on a heat diffuser mat for 12 minutes, or until the underneath is set. The top should still be slightly runny. Then pop the pan under a preheated grill for 1 minute just to set the surface, but don't let it brown.
Or After an initial 3–4 minutes on the hob, transfer the pan to a preheated oven at 170°C/gas mark 3 for 15–20 minutes, or until the frittata is just set. I prefer this method.

To turn out the frittata, slide a palette knife underneath to free it from the pan and carefully slide it onto a warm plate.

To serve, cut into wedges and arrange some rocket leaves with a drizzle of extra virgin olive oil on top. Accompany with a good green salad or perhaps a tomato and basil leaf salad.

A tasty little supper in a frying pan. I use a lovely hand-forged pan for this one, which I like to bring to the table – but if you'd rather not, you can simply slide the contents onto a warm serving plate and enjoy.

Fried eggs *with red pepper & chorizo*

- 2 tablespoons extra virgin olive oil
- 1 small onion, finely sliced
- 1 medium red pepper, deseeded and cut into 2cm squares
- ½–1 red chilli, deseeded and thinly sliced
- 4 organic, free-range eggs
- a pinch of pul biber (optional)
- 1 avocado, peeled, stoned and cut into 2.5cm chunks
- 2 tablespoons diced chorizo
- 2 tablespoons sliced spring onions
- 2 tablespoons chopped coriander
- flaky sea salt and freshly ground black pepper

Heat the oil in a 30cm non-stick frying pan over a medium heat and add the onion, red pepper and chilli. Season well with salt and pepper. Cover and cook for 4–5 minutes, stirring occasionally, until almost soft. Transfer to a plate, wipe out the pan and pop it back on the hob with a generous layer of extra virgin olive oil.

Crack the eggs into the pan, and season generously with salt, freshly ground black pepper and a pinch of pul biber. Cover the pan with a lid and cook for 4–5 minutes until the whites are set, but the yolks are still nicely soft.

Sprinkle the onion, pepper and chilli mixture over the top and add some chunks of avocado and diced chorizo. Scatter over the spring onions and coriander and serve as soon as possible.

Other good sprinkles

SMOKED MACKEREL OR SALMON
Follow the recipe above, replacing the avocado and chorizo with 2 tablespoons of diced smoked salmon. Replace the coriander with 2 tablespoons of chopped dill.

TOMATO & CHERVIL
Follow the recipe above, replacing the chorizo with 2–3 tablespoons of diced very ripe tomato and replace the coriander with 2 tablespoons of chopped chervil.

POTATO & OLIVE
Follow the recipe above, replacing the chorizo with 125g diced cooked potatoes and the avocado with 6 pitted Kalamata olives.

SERVES 2

For many of us, scrambled eggs are the perennial standby – a tasty breakfast or supper dish, made in minutes, delicious unadorned but also a vehicle for all sorts of morsels from the fridge. Soft folds of scrambled egg are rare indeed. For perfection, really fresh free-range eggs are essential. Perfectly scrambled eggs need no further embellishment, except perhaps some hot thin toast and lots of freshly cracked pepper. I adore the luxurious combination of Lough Neagh smoked eel and softly scrambled eggs, but smoked mackerel or wild smoked salmon also work beautifully.

Scrambled eggs *with smoked fish & chervil*

- 4 organic, free-range eggs
- 2 tablespoons creamy milk or single cream
- a knob of butter
- 225g Irish smoked salmon, mackerel or eel, cut into 2cm dice
- 1 tablespoon chopped chervil, plus a few extra sprigs to garnish
- 1 tablespoon grated Parmesan cheese
- flaky sea salt and freshly ground black pepper

Break the eggs into a bowl, add the milk or cream and season with salt and pepper. Whisk thoroughly until the whites and yolks are well mixed.

Put a blob of butter into a cold 22cm low-sided, heavy-based saucepan, pour in the egg mixture and stir continuously over a low heat, preferably with a flat-bottomed wooden spoon, until the eggs have scrambled into soft creamy curds. Carefully fold in the smoked fish and chopped chervil.

Serve immediately on warm plates with a sprinkling of grated Parmesan and a few sprigs of fresh chervil on top. Accompany with lots of hot buttered sourdough toast or fresh soda bread. (Note: If the plates are too hot, the scrambled egg can actually overcook between the hob and the table.)

Delicious morsels to add to scrambled eggs

FINES HERBES

Follow the main recipe, replacing the smoked fish and chervil with 1 tablespoon of mixed fresh herbs, such as chives, flat-leaf parsley, tarragon, basil, chervil, coriander, dill or tansy.

CHILLI OR HARISSA

Follow the main recipe, replacing the smoked fish and chervil with ½–1 teaspoon of diced or sliced red chilli, or harissa and a herb of your choice.

SPICES

Follow the main recipe, replacing the smoked fish and chervil with ½–1 teaspoon of ground cumin and ½–1 teaspoon of ground coriander. Add or omit the sprinkling of Parmesan as you wish.

CHEESE

Follow the main recipe, replacing the smoked fish and chervil with 2–4 tablespoons of grated cheese, such as Cheddar, Monterey Jack, Gruyère, Parmesan or Pecorino.

'NDUJA, CHORIZO OR BACON

Cut 50g bacon or chorizo into 5mm dice and fry gently until the oil begins to release. Follow the main recipe, replacing the smoked fish with the 'nduja, fried bacon or chorizo (the 'nduja doesn't need to be cooked). Add or omit the Parmesan as you wish.

SPRING ONIONS OR CHIVES

Follow the main recipe, replacing the smoked fish and chervil with 2 tablespoons of chopped spring onions or chives.

SORREL, SPINACH OR KALE

Blanch 225g sorrel, spinach or kale in boiling water for 2–3 minutes, refresh under cold running water, drain thoroughly and finely chop. Follow the main recipe, replacing the smoked fish and chervil with the sorrel, spinach or kale.

FORAGED GREENS

Follow the recipe above, replacing the smoked fish and chervil with 225g chopped wild garlic, sorrel, dandelion or watercress, or a mixture.

CHANTERELLES OR YELLOW LEG MUSHROOMS

Fry 110g mushrooms in ½–1 tablespoon of butter and season well. Follow the main recipe, replacing the smoked fish and chervil with the mushrooms.

MASALA SCRAMBLED EGG

Heat the butter over a medium heat. Add 50g finely diced onion and ½ teaspoon of grated fresh ginger and sauté until the onion is soft. Add ½–1 diced red chilli, 2 very ripe tomatoes, peeled and chopped, 2 teaspoons of ground cumin, 1 tablespoon of chopped coriander, ⅛ teaspoon of ground turmeric and stir for a few seconds. Reduce the heat right down, add the whisked eggs and scramble as before. Garnish with a few sprigs of fresh coriander.

SERVES 6

Another one-pot gem that makes a perfect lunch or supper dish. I bake this soufflé until golden and puffy in a shallow sauté pan instead of the traditional soufflé dish. The cheese needs to be really tasty. Pretty pink or purple thyme flowers are so lovely sprinkled over the top just before serving.

Goat's cheese & thyme leaf soufflé

- 300ml double cream
- 300ml whole milk
- 1 small onion, quartered
- sprig of thyme, a few flat-leaf parsley stalks and a little scrap of bay leaf
- 75g butter
- 40g plain flour
- 5 organic, free-range eggs, separated
- 110g crumbled goat's cheese (I use St. Tola or Ardsallagh farmhouse goat's cheese)
- 75g Gruyère cheese, grated
- 50g mature Coolea* or Parmigiano Reggiano, grated
- a good pinch of sea salt, freshly ground black pepper, cayenne and nutmeg
- 2 teaspoons fresh thyme leaves and thyme flowers, in season, to garnish

*Good to know

Coolea is an award-winning Irish Gouda-type farmhouse cheese.

Preheat the oven to 230°C/gas mark 8.

Pour the cream and milk into a heavy-based pan, add the onion and herbs and bring almost to the boil. Turn off the heat and set aside to infuse for 15 minutes or so.

Melt the butter in a sauté pan, add the flour and cook for a minute or two. Strain the hot, creamy milk into the pan, whisking continuously as it comes to the boil and thickens. Remove from the heat and set aside to cool slightly.

Beat in the egg yolks, goat's cheese, Gruyère and most of the Coolea (or Parmesan) and season to taste with salt, freshly ground black pepper, cayenne and nutmeg.

In a separate bowl, whisk the egg whites until stiff peaks form and gently fold in the cheese sauce to make a loose consistency. Scatter the thyme leaves over the surface and sprinkle with the remaining Coolea (or Parmesan).

Cook in the hot oven for 20–25 minutes until the sides and top of the soufflé are nicely puffed up and golden – the centre should still be creamy. Garnish with thyme flowers, if available.

Serve immediately on warm plates with a good green salad.

This version of eggy bread comes from Kolkata, where street vendors set up their street food stalls on Park Street and Fairlie Place in the business district at noon each day, collectively they will feed the hundreds of workers who pour out of their offices in search of tasty nourishing foods – this simple snack is filling and super delicious.

Indian French toast

- 4 thickish slices of good white bread
- 3–4 organic, free-range eggs
- 1 small onion, finely chopped
- 1 green chilli, deseeded and chopped
- 4 tablespoons chopped coriander
- rock or sea salt and freshly ground black pepper
- olive oil, for frying

First lightly toast the bread (in Kolkata it is grilled over charcoal). Whisk the eggs in a flattish dish; add a pinch of salt, finely chopped onion, green chilli and coriander.

Dip one slice of bread into the egg, then flip over to make sure it is saturated on both sides.

Warm a little oil in a large frying pan until sizzling. Slap in the soaked bread.

Repeat with the remaining three slices and use up all the egg. Cook until crisp and golden on both sides. Cut into quarters, sprinkle generously with salt and serve.

POULTRY

At Ballymaloe, we're all addicted to Chicken Noodle Soup and this Thai version is a perennial favourite. We grow Thai basil in our greenhouse, but Genovese basil is also good here.

Thai chicken & *noodle coconut broth*

- 175g flat rice noodles
- 1 x 400ml tin best-quality coconut milk
- 500ml homemade chicken stock
- 1 heaped tablespoon grated fresh ginger
- 1 fresh red chilli, finely sliced
- 1 tablespoon chopped coriander
- 1–2 tablespoons fish sauce
- 2 organic, free-range chicken breasts, boned and skinned
- 1 handful of fresh Thai basil leaves

TO SERVE
- 4 tablespoons thinly sliced spring onion
- coriander leaves

Pour boiling water over the noodles in a bowl. Cover and leave to sit for about 10 minutes. Drain and rinse immediately under cold water. Cut the noodles into 2cm lengths. Leave in the colander until you are ready to serve the soup.

Put the coconut milk, chicken stock, ginger, chilli, coriander and fish sauce into a medium saucepan over a medium heat. Bring to the boil and simmer gently for 10 minutes, then reduce the heat so the broth is barely bubbling.

Meanwhile, cut the chicken breasts across into 2mm slivers. Add the sliced chicken to the broth and cook very gently for 3–4 minutes until the chicken slices change colour and are just cooked through. Adjust the seasoning, adding a little extra fish sauce if necessary. Throw in the basil leaves and leave to stand for a few minutes.

Pour a kettle of boiling water over the noodles in the colander and drain well.

Warm 4–6 wide deep bowls and divide the noodles between them. Top with the chicken and ladle over the hot coconut broth. Serve at once, scattered with spring onions and fresh coriander. A few lime wedges can be nice as well.

If asparagus is in season, slice 4–6 trimmed spears at an angle and add them to the pot 4–5 minutes before the end of the cooking time for extra deliciousness in this spring pot. Florets of Romanesco in season are another of my top additions to this dish.

A spring chicken *in a pot*

- 6 large organic, free-range chicken thighs or drumsticks
- 2 tablespoons extra virgin olive oil
- 2 medium onions, roughly chopped
- 450ml homemade chicken stock
- 12 small new potatoes
- a sprig of thyme
- 1 Hispi or spring cabbage, finely sliced
- 150g peas, podded weight
- 1 tablespoon chopped tarragon
- 4 spring onions, sliced
- 2 tablespoons coarsely chopped flat-leaf parsley
- flaky sea salt and freshly ground black pepper
- 4–5 tablespoons double cream or crème fraîche (optional)

Season the chicken pieces well with salt and pepper.

Heat the olive oil in a 4.2-litre heavy casserole over a high-ish heat, add the chicken and brown them lightly on all sides.

Stir in the onions, then add the well-flavoured stock, potatoes and a nice sprig of thyme. Season with salt and pepper. Bring to the boil, then cover with a lid and simmer for 30 minutes.

Remove the thyme sprig, add the cabbage and simmer gently for a further 5–6 minutes, uncovered. Add the peas and tarragon and cook for another couple of minutes. Stir in half of the spring onions and parsley, saving the rest to scatter over the top. Season to taste, add the cream or crème fraîche (if using) and serve.

There are many versions of this Georgian pheasant recipe. We particularly love to make it with wild pheasant, which has lots of gamey flavour, and walnuts from the tree at the end of the garden that I planted myself over twenty-five years ago and am inordinately proud of.

Faisinjan

- 2 plump pheasants, each cut into 4 portions
- 2 tablespoons extra virgin olive oil
- 1 onion, chopped
- 1 x 5–7.5cm cinnamon stick
- 225g shelled walnuts, finely chopped but gritty
- 3 tablespoons pomegranate syrup
- 450ml homemade chicken or pheasant stock
- 2 tablespoons chopped flat-leaf parsley
- flaky sea salt, freshly ground black pepper and sugar, to taste

Season the pheasant pieces with salt and pepper.

Heat the oil in a 25cm frying pan over a medium heat and brown the pheasant pieces on all sides. Transfer to a plate.

Add the onion to the pan and fry until pale golden brown, stirring regularly to prevent burning. Reduce the heat and add the cinnamon stick and walnuts. Cook gently for a few minutes, stirring, then add the pomegranate syrup and stock. Bring to the boil, stirring.

Add the pheasant pieces back to the pan, then cover the pan with a lid and simmer gently for 30 minutes. Uncover and continue to cook over a gentle heat for 15–30 minutes until the meat is very tender and the sauce is thick. Taste and add more salt or pepper and a little sugar, if necessary, to balance the sauce. It should taste sweet and sour.

To serve, sprinkle with the chopped parsley and accompany with a good green salad and a big bowl of mashed potato or rice, if you wish.

- 1 x approx. 2kg organic chicken

- **2kg selection of chunky vegetables of your choice, such as:**
  carrots, peeled and cut into 4cm chunks
  parsnips, peeled and cut into 4cm chunks
  pumpkin or butternut squash, peeled and cut into 4cm chunks (optional)
  Jerusalem artichokes, peeled and cut into 4cm chunks
  red onions, peeled and cut into quarters or sixths depending on size
  beetroot, peeled and cut into 4cm chunks
  celeriac, peeled and cut into 4cm chunks
  leeks, cut into 2.5cm slices
- extra virgin olive oil
- 8 whole garlic cloves, unpeeled
- sea salt and freshly ground black pepper
- 2 tablespoons rosemary or thyme leaves, plus extra fresh herbs, such as chervil, flat-leaf parsley, chives, to garnish

FOR THE MARINADE
- 1 tablespoon rosemary, chopped
- 4 garlic cloves, crushed
- 1 teaspoon freshly ground black pepper
- ½ teaspoon chilli flakes (pul biber or Espelette pepper)
- ½ tablespoon freshly squeezed organic lemon juice
- 4 tablespoons extra virgin olive oil
- 1 teaspoon flaky sea salt or more if needed

- Gremolata or Pangrattato (optional accompaniment – see pages 70 and 101)

SERVES 6–8

When you master this simple technique, it creates so many possibilities — a plump chicken, duck or even a turkey, will roast in half the time. I have so much fun doing riffs on this recipe — how about Moroccan or Tunisian, Nordic, Georgian, Persian or Baltic flavours — to whet your appetite just a little. At its simplest, just drizzle the skin side of your bird with extra virgin olive oil and scatter with freshly chopped rosemary or thyme leaves. Maybe add a sprinkling of pul biber or slather the skin with harissa or smoked paprika oil, or a masala oil to introduce a taste of India. Roasting the chicken over the tray of chunky root vegetables allows the juices and chicken fat to enhance the taste of the vegetables even further. Depending on the flavour, you may want to sprinkle it with gremolata or pangrattato, optional but a delicious addition.

Spatchcock chicken
with rosemary & chilli oil

First spatchcock the chicken. To spatchcock or butterfly the bird. Remove the wishbone from the neck end (save for stock). Lay the chicken, breast side down, on a chopping board. Use a poultry shears to remove the back bone by cutting along both sides (chop the bone into 4 or 5 pieces and use to make a stock for gravy later). Then flip the chicken, breast side up, and rotate the legs so the drumsticks point outwards. Press down firmly on the breast bone several times to flatten the bird. Tuck the wing tips behind the breast to make a neat shape. Trim the excess neck fat from the bird and add to the stock. If this all seems too much to tackle, ask your butcher to spatchcock the chicken for you.

Next make the marinade. Mix the rosemary, garlic, pepper, chilli flakes, lemon juice and extra virgin olive oil together in a bowl. Just before cooking, brush the chicken both inside and out with the marinade. Put the chicken, skin side up on a wire rack. Sprinkle with flaky sea salt and allow to absorb the flavours for as long as you can spare, at least 30 minutes.

Meanwhile, preheat the oven 180°C/gas mark 4.

Slide the rack into the oven and cook the chicken, skin side up, for about 45 minutes.

Meanwhile, prepare the selection of vegetables. Transfer to a roasting tin with the garlic cloves and drizzle with extra virgin olive oil. Season generously with salt and pepper. Sprinkle with chopped rosemary or thyme leaves. Toss well until the vegetables are evenly coated. Slide the roasting tin of vegetables or just potatoes underneath the rack with the chicken and cook for 20–35 minutes or until the vegetables are soft and slightly caramelised. Make sure the chicken is fully cooked through.

To serve, carve into portions and serve on top of the roast vegetables or potatoes scattered with some freshly chopped herbs - chervil, parsley, chives – or the gremolata or pangrattato, if you wish. Serve with a good green salad.

SERVES 6

I sometimes use scraps from the chicken carcass from the stockpot for this recipe, but you could use raw or cooked chicken (either brown or white meat).
Provide a platter of good things alongside – avocado, tomato, red onion, green chilli, fresh coriander, tortilla chips and segments of fresh lime – for your family and friends to add to their broth as they choose.

Mexican chicken broth
with many good things

- 1.8 litres well-flavoured and well-skimmed homemade chicken stock
- 225g uncooked or cooked, shredded chicken (I prefer to use brown meat)
- flaky sea salt and freshly ground black pepper

TO SERVE
- 6 medium red tomatoes, cut into 1cm dice
- 2–3 ripe Hass avocados, cut into 1.5cm dice
- 2 medium red onions, cut into 1cm dice
- 2 green Serrano or Jalapeño chillies, thinly sliced
- 3 organic limes, cut into wedges
- 3–4 soft corn tortillas or a large bag of high-quality tortilla chips
- 4–6 tablespoons coarsely chopped coriander leaves

Put the chicken stock into a wide 2.5-litre saucepan and bring to the boil. Taste and season with salt and pepper – the stock should have a full rich flavour, otherwise the soup will be bland and insipid.

Just before serving, add the shredded chicken to the hot broth and poach gently so it doesn't toughen. Cooked chicken just needs to be heated through in the broth. Raw white meat will take 2–3 minutes to cook and brown meat a little longer – 4–6 minutes. Season to taste.

I like to bring the soup to the table in a soup tureen. To serve, ladle into soup bowls and serve with your chosen accompaniments.

This roast cauliflower is delicious on its own but also pretty irresistible with some spicy chicken drumsticks. Look out for pul biber, not too hot but really aromatic. I fell in love with them on my first trip to Turkey.

Roast cauliflower *with saffron & bay leaves* & crispy chicken

- 4–8 organic, free-range chicken thighs or drumsticks, depending on size
- extra virgin olive oil
- ½–1 teaspoon rosemary, chopped
- 2 pinches of saffron strands
- 1 large or 2 small cauliflowers (approx. 1kg), leaves snapped off*, head broken into small florets, stalk roughly chopped
- 2 medium onions, finely sliced
- 1 tablespoon pul biber or a good pinch of dried chilli flakes
- 3 bay leaves
- 50g sultanas, soaked in hot water to plump up
- 50g almonds, coarsely chopped
- flaky sea salt and freshly ground black pepper

TO SERVE
- 2 tablespoons roughly chopped flat-leaf parsley
- 4 spring onions, sliced on the diagonal

Preheat the oven to 200°C/gas mark 6.

Slash the chicken drumsticks. Drizzle with a little extra virgin olive oil. Season with salt and pepper. Sprinkle with chopped rosemary, toss and arrange in a single layer in a roasting tin. Roast for 30–45 minutes, depending on size, while you prepare the cauliflower.

Put the saffron into a little bowl, cover it with a couple of teaspoons of boiling water and leave it to steep. Put the cauliflower, onions, chilli flakes and bay leaves into a bowl and season with salt and pepper.

Once the saffron has steeped, add to the cauliflower mixture with the drained sultanas and almonds. Transfer to the roasting tin and cover loosely with parchment paper to protect from burning. Bake for 20 minutes.

Remove the parchment and roast for a further 10–15 minutes until the edges are nicely caramelised, the cauliflower is tender and the chicken is cooked. Turn into a shallow serving dish.

Sprinkle with the chopped parsley and spring onion. Serve.

*Good to know
The leaves are also delicious roasted, add them a little later.

A quickie that can be put together in a few minutes using your favourite curry powder. For the purpose of this one-pot book, we experimented by adding the rice to the curry close to the end of cooking. It works brilliantly and is super delicious.

Coconut curry chicken & *rice*

- 900g organic, free-range chicken breast or thigh meat, cut into 1cm chunks
- 25g your favourite curry powder
- 3 tablespoons extra virgin olive oil
- 150g onions, thinly sliced
- 2 garlic cloves, crushed
- 600ml coconut milk
- 1 x 400g tin of plum tomatoes, diced, and their juice
- 1 teaspoon granulated sugar
- 300g basmati rice, soaked for 15–30 minutes in cold water and drained
- flaky sea salt and freshly ground black pepper

TO SERVE
- 1 lime, cut into wedges
- chopped coriander
- 4–6 spring onions, sliced on the diagonal

Season the chicken with salt and pepper. Mix together the curry power and oil in a small bowl. Heat a large saucepan, approx. 25cm in diameter and 10cm deep, over a medium heat, add the curry oil mixture and stir for a minute or two. Add the onions and garlic and cook gently for 3 minutes until they start to colour.

Add the chicken chunks and toss lightly to coat them with the curry oil mixture. Reduce the heat, cover with a lid and simmer for 3–4 minutes, stirring occasionally.

Pour in the coconut milk, add the diced tomatoes and their juice and season with salt, freshly ground black pepper and sugar. Bring to the boil, stirring, and then cover the pan with a lid and simmer gently until the chicken is cooked. Chicken breast should take 5–6 minutes; thigh meat will take a little longer, about 10–15 minutes. Sprinkle in the rice 6–8 minutes before the end of cooking. Remove the pan from the heat and set aside for 7 minutes, tightly covered with the lid, to allow the rice to swell.

To serve, squeeze over some lime juice to taste and sprinkle with fresh coriander and lots of spring onion. Accompany with a bowl of organic salad leaves.

This versatile one-pot winner also works with either drumsticks or thighs. Allow an extra 5–10 minutes for drumsticks in the oven – 35–45 minutes in total. For best results with chicken thighs, slash each thigh three times right down to the bone to speed up the cooking time and encourage them to soak up all of the flavours.

Chicken wings *with tomato, pepper & harissa potatoes*

- 24 organic, free-range chicken wings, weighing approx. 1.4kg
- 1 heaped teaspoon chopped rosemary leaves
- 1 teaspoon thyme leaves
- 3½ tablespoons extra virgin olive oil
- 1 tablespoon harissa paste or smoked paprika
- 500g onions, cut into 1cm slices
- 1kg potatoes, peeled and cut into 7mm slices
- 450g red peppers, deseeded and cut into 2cm squares
- 1 head of garlic, divided into cloves
- 2 sprigs of rosemary
- 2 generous sprigs of thyme
- 450g ripe tomatoes, cored and halved
- 1–2 teaspoons honey
- flaky sea salt and freshly ground black pepper

TO SERVE
- flat-leaf parsley or coriander sprigs
- a sprinkling of smoked paprika

Preheat the oven to 230°C/gas mark 8.

Tip the chicken wings into a large bowl and add the rosemary, thyme, ½ tablespoon of extra virgin olive oil and lots of sea salt. Rub the herby oil into the chicken wings and set aside.

Mix the harissa paste or smoked paprika with 3 tablespoons of extra virgin olive oil in a little bowl. Set aside.

Tip the sliced onions and potatoes into an approx. 38 x 30 x 3cm roasting tin. Add the red pepper and whole garlic cloves and drizzle with the harissa/paprika paste. Season, throw in the sprigs of rosemary and thyme and toss well to coat the vegetables. Spread out the vegetables in a single layer. Arrange the tomatoes on top of the vegetables. Season each tomato with salt and pepper, a drizzle of honey and the remaining harissa/paprika paste.

Arrange the chicken wings in a single layer on an oven rack and slide into the oven. Slide the tray of vegetables into the oven, under the chicken wings so that the juices from the wings drip onto the vegetables. Roast the chicken wings for 30–35 minutes, turning them halfway through to crisp up on both sides. Once the wings are cooked through and crisp, remove them from the oven and set aside to rest.

Increase the temperature to 250°C/gas mark 10 and roast the vegetables for a further 10 minutes until nicely caramelised. Remove the vegetables from the oven and lay the crispy wings on top. Sprinkle with the coriander sprigs and flat-leaf parsley and dust with a little more smoked paprika, if you fancy. Serve straight from the roasting tray.

Tumble all of the ingredients together in a bowl,
season them well and toss them into a roasting tin
for an irresistible one-dish supper.

Chicken supper in a dish *with aioli*

- 2kg potatoes, such as Golden Wonder or Kerr's Pink
- 225–275g medium onions, sliced into rings
- 8–10 large organic, free-range chicken legs, separated into thighs and drumsticks
- 1 large head of garlic, separated into cloves
- 1–2 tablespoons sweet or smoked paprika (or a mixture of both)
- 2 tablespoons chopped marjoram
- 3 tablespoons extra virgin olive oil
- juice of 1 organic lemon
- flaky sea salt and freshly ground black pepper

TO SERVE
- 3–4 large ripe tomatoes
- a dash of balsamic vinegar, to taste
- a dash of honey or sugar, to taste
- 3–4 sprigs of flat-leaf parsley
- Aioli (page 96)

Preheat the oven to 230°C/gas mark 8.

Peel the potatoes and cut them into chunky wedges. Put them into a large bowl with the sliced onion rings, chicken pieces and garlic cloves and sprinkle over the paprika, marjoram and plenty of salt and pepper. Drizzle generously with the extra virgin olive oil and squeeze over the lemon juice. Toss thoroughly to coat the potatoes and the chicken in the flavourings. Spread in a single layer over a large roasting tray or a large gratin dish, approx. 35 x 40cm.

Roast for 15–20 minutes, then reduce the heat to a moderate 180°C/gas mark 4 for a further 45 minutes or until the potatoes are golden and crisp at the edges and the chicken skin is sticky and irresistible. Check the chicken is cooked close to the bone; it may take a little longer.

Coarsely chop the tomatoes and place them in a small bowl. Season to taste with salt, freshly ground black pepper, balsamic vinegar and honey (or sugar). Stir in the parsley. Sprinkle the tomato mixture over the hot chicken just as it comes out of the oven.

Accompany with the aioli and a salad of organic leaves anointed with an extra virgin olive oil and lemon juice dressing.

This is a favourite way to cook pork in Italy, but the technique also works brilliantly with chicken, rose veal or lamb. There is honestly no point in attempting this recipe if you cannot find a really good free-range bird. Cooking in milk produces the most delicious curdy liquid and the lactic acid in the milk has a tenderising and moistening effect on the meat. Here, I've cooked the potatoes or rice in the milky juices – you can just imagine how delicious it all tastes.

Chicken *poached in milk*

- 1.8kg organic, free-range chicken
- 1 tablespoon extra virgin olive oil
- thinly sliced peel from 1 organic lemon
- 1 teaspoon lightly crushed coriander seeds (or a small handful of fresh sage leaves)
- 4 garlic cloves, halved
- approx. 900ml whole milk
- a small bunch of marjoram
- 6–8 potatoes, peeled and halved or quartered, depending on size
  or 200–225g basmati rice, soaked for 15–30 minutes in cold water and drained
- flaky sea salt and freshly ground black pepper
- a few sprigs of chervil, to serve

Joint the chicken into 10 pieces and season generously with salt and pepper.

Heat 1 tablespoon olive oil in a 3.2-litre/25cm casserole over a medium heat and brown the chicken pieces well on all sides. Remove them to a plate, then pour off the hot fat in the pan and discard.

Return the pan to a medium heat and add the lemon peel, coriander seeds (or sage) and garlic. Return the chicken pieces to the pan and pour in the milk so that it comes about halfway up the meat. Add the marjoram and bring to the boil.

Partially cover the pan with a lid and simmer gently over a low heat for about 50 minutes, by which time the milk should have formed a golden skin. The liquid should simmer very gently all the time. The whole object of this exercise is to allow the milk to reduce slowly and form delicious, pale coffee-coloured 'curds' while the meat cooks.

If using potatoes, add them about 30 minutes into the start of the cooking time, scraping down any milk that has stuck to the sides of the pan at the same time. (If using rice, add after 45 minutes, scraping down any milk that has stuck to the sides of the pan. Cook for a further 6–7 minutes over a low heat, then remove the pan from the heat, cover, and set aside for 5–10 minutes to allow the rice to swell.)

Serve the chicken with the precious curds spooned carefully over the top alongside the potatoes (or rice) and a scattering of chervil.

SERVES 12

Crisp leaves of Little Gem lettuce provide the perfect scoops for chunks of tender chicken, drizzled with creamy Caesar dressing. This one is best served while the chicken is still a little warm.

Roast chicken salad *with* avocado & Caesar dressing

- 1 x 1.8–2kg organic, free-range chicken
- 2 organic lemons
- 2 tablespoons extra virgin olive oil
- 1 tablespoon clear honey
- 6 Little Gem lettuces
- 4 avocados
- 2 handfuls of watercress or wood sorrel
- flaky sea salt, freshly ground black pepper and pul biber
- a handful of marigold petals, to garnish

Preheat the oven to 180°C/gas mark 4.

Season the inside of the chicken with salt and pepper. Prick the lemons all over with a skewer and put them inside the chicken cavity. Tie the legs together and place the chicken in a medium roasting tin, approx. 33 x 30cm. Drizzle the skin with the extra virgin olive oil.

Roast the chicken for 1½ hours, then brush the skin with honey, season with salt, freshly ground black pepper and a sprinkling of pul biber and return to the oven for a further 15 minutes until the chicken is well-cooked and golden brown. Remove from the roasting tin and set aside to cool.

FOR THE CAESAR DRESSING

- 1 x 50g tin of anchovies
- 2 organic, free-range egg yolks
- 1 garlic clove, crushed
- 2 tablespoons freshly squeezed organic lemon juice
- a generous pinch of English mustard powder
- ½ teaspoon sea salt
- ½–1 tablespoon Worcestershire sauce
- ½–1 tablespoon Tabasco sauce
- 175ml sunflower oil
- 50ml extra virgin olive oil
- 50ml cold water

Meanwhile, make the dressing. I usually whizz up the Caesar dressing in a food processor, but you could also make it very quickly by hand. Drain the anchovies and crush them lightly with a fork. Place them in a food processor or medium-sized bowl with the egg yolks, garlic, lemon juice, mustard powder, salt, Worcestershire and Tabasco sauces. Whisk all of the ingredients together and then gradually start to whisk in the oils, adding them very slowly at first and then a little faster as the emulsion starts to form. Finally whisk in the water to make a spreadable consistency. Season to taste: this dressing should be highly flavoured.

To serve, separate the leaves from the lettuces and arrange them over two platters. Remove each breast carefully from the chicken in one piece. Pull the meat from the legs and wings and tear it into chunky pieces. (Save the carcass to make stock.) Season the meat with salt and pepper. Cut each breast into 6 pieces, keeping the skin attached. Put a small spoonful of the brown meat into each lettuce leaf and top with a slice of breast meat. Halve, stone and peel the avocado, then cut into quarters or sixths. Tuck a piece of avocado in amongst the chicken.

Just before serving, drizzle a little dressing over each piece of chicken. Garnish with a sprig of watercress or wood sorrel and sprinkle with the marigold petals, if available. Serve soon.

Any remaining dressing can be served as an accompaniment or stored in a lidded jar in the fridge for 10 days.

Another dish that family and friends love me to cook
for them. A whole roasting tray of crispy chicken and
potatoes, perfumed with rosemary and thyme leaves.
My lips are smacking just thinking about it.

Roman chicken & chips
with rosemary & thyme

- 2kg organic, free-range chicken thighs,
  drumsticks and wings
- 2–3 tablespoons thyme leaves
- 1–2 tablespoons chopped rosemary
- 1.1kg (about 10 large) potatoes
- extra virgin olive oil, to drizzle
- 250g onions, sliced
- flaky sea salt and freshly ground
  black pepper

Preheat the oven to 230°C/gas mark 8.

Season the chicken heavily with salt and pepper. Put into a
large bowl and scatter with the thyme leaves and chopped
rosemary, reserving some for the potatoes. Toss well.

Peel the potatoes and cut into 1cm-thick chips. Dry and
season well with salt, freshly ground black pepper and the
reserved thyme and chopped rosemary. Add to the bowl
with the chicken. Drizzle with extra virgin olive oil and toss
once again.

Scatter the sliced onions over the base of a roasting tin,
approx. 37 x 31 x 2cm, or two smaller tins approx. 30 x 20 x
2.5cm. Arrange the chicken and potatoes haphazardly on top,
making sure that the potatoes are popping up. Drizzle with a
little more olive oil.

Roast for 45 minutes–1 hour or until the chicken is cooked
through and the chips are crispy at the edges. (Organic
chicken pieces are larger, so cooking time can be up to
1¼ hours.)

Serve from the tin, family style, with a good green salad and
several vegetables of your choice, if you wish.

*Good to know

One can add a little hot homemade chicken stock
at the end if the dish needs a little more juice.

Molley is an Indian dish which uses coconut and spices and is often made with fish, but here these flavours transform minced turkey into a totally irresistible one-pot meal. Gary Masterson, one of our tutors at the Ballymaloe Cookery School, shared this recipe and the one opposite with me.

Turkey molley

FOR THE MEATBALLS

- 2 tablespoons extra virgin olive oil
- 110g onions, finely chopped
- 250g minced turkey
- 75g grated coconut
- 10g fresh ginger, grated
- 1 teaspoon white wine vinegar
- ½ teaspoon sea salt

FOR THE SAUCE

- 3 tablespoons extra virgin olive oil
- 200g onions, finely chopped
- 6 garlic cloves, crushed
- 2 red chillies, finely diced
- 1 level teaspoon ground turmeric
- 5 medium tomatoes, quartered
- 200g cauliflower, broken into
  1–2cm florets
- 6 garlic cloves, sliced
- 10g fresh ginger, grated
- ½ teaspoon sea salt
- 2 teaspoons white wine vinegar
- 200ml coconut milk
- 3 green chillies, slit

FOR THE BANANA & YOGURT RAITA

- approx. 25g raisins or sultanas
- 15g blanched slivered almonds
- 3–4 green cardamom pods
- 90ml natural yogurt
- 40ml double cream
- 40ml soured cream
- 1 dessertspoon local honey
- 2–4 firm ripe bananas, depending on size
- a pinch of salt

First prepare the meatballs. Heat the oil over a medium heat in a 30cm frying pan and gently fry the onion for 4–5 minutes until soft. Set aside to cool.

Combine the minced turkey, coconut, ginger, fried onion, vinegar and salt in a large bowl. Shape into 16 meatballs the size of a small lime. Transfer to a plate, cover with clingfilm and set aside to firm up in the fridge for about an hour.

Meanwhile, make the raita. Pour boiling water over the raisins or sultanas and set aside for 10 minutes. Toast the almonds (watch them: they burn really easily). Remove the seeds from the cardamom pods, crush in a pestle and mortar. Mix the yogurt with the creams and cardamom, add the honey, taste and add more if needed. Add the drained raisins. Slice the bananas, season with a pinch of salt and add to the yogurt base. Turn into a serving bowl and scatter with the toasted almonds, chill for an hour if possible.

To make the sauce, heat the oil in the frying pan over a lowish heat and fry the onion, crushed garlic, chilli, turmeric and tomatoes for 4–5 minutes until softened. Add the cauliflower, sliced garlic, ginger, salt and vinegar, and cook for a further 3–4 minutes, stirring. Pour in the coconut milk, stir gently and bring to the boil.

Tuck the meatballs into the sauce, then cover with a lid and simmer gently for about 15 minutes or until the meatballs are cooked through. Remove the lid, add the green chillies and cook for a further 5 minutes until the sauce thickens. Season to taste.

Accompany with banana and cardamom raita, and some tomato chutney and flatbreads, if you wish.

These spices will transform the mince into something irresistible, to scoop up with fresh lettuce leaves. Minced chicken can also be used; I prefer the brown meat but, of course, white meat is delicious too – just bear in mind that it needs a shorter cooking time.

Gary's Asian turkey lettuce wraps

- 2 tablespoons vegetable oil
- 30g fresh ginger, grated
- 2 garlic cloves, crushed
- 2 red chillies, deseeded and finely chopped
- 500g minced turkey (I use brown meat, but use white if you prefer)
- 4 kaffir lime leaves, shredded
- 50g palm sugar or soft light brown sugar
- juice of 1 organic lime
- 2 tablespoons fish sauce

ACCOMPANIMENTS
- 3–4 handfuls of Iceberg lettuce or 6 Little Gems halved
- a good handful of mint leaves
- a handful of coriander leaves
- 2–3 spring shallots, finely sliced on the diagonal
- a handful of toasted peanuts or cashews, roughly chopped
- 1 organic lime, cut into wedges

Heat the oil over a high heat in a large (26cm) frying pan. Add the ginger, garlic and chillies and stir-fry for a minute or two to release their flavours. Add the minced turkey and cook over a high heat until it starts to colour, breaking it up with a wooden spoon as you go.

Add the kaffir lime leaves, sprinkle in the sugar, squeeze in the lime juice and add 1 tablespoon of the fish sauce. Reduce the heat and cook everything down for 5–10 minutes until the mince is sticky and delicious. Season to taste with the remaining fish sauce, if necessary.

To serve, transfer the mince to a serving bowl and accompany with little bowls of lettuce, herbs, shallots, peanuts or cashews and lime wedges so that everyone can assemble their own little parcels.

This wonderful Moroccan dish, which Claudia Roden made for us when she was guest chef at the school, derives its name from the tomatoes in which it cooks (there are mountains of them that reduce to a thick sauce) and from the honey, which comes in at the end.

Moroccan chicken tagine
with tomatoes & honey

- 6 organic, free-range chicken legs
- 3 tablespoons extra virgin olive oil
- 225g onions, diced
- 1 garlic clove, crushed
- 1 teaspoon ground cinnamon
- 1 teaspoon grated fresh ginger
- a pinch of saffron threads
- 1.3kg very ripe tomatoes, peeled and chopped, or tinned chopped tomatoes
- 2 tablespoons honey
- flaky sea salt and freshly ground black pepper

FOR THE GARNISH
- 50g blanched almonds, toasted
- 1 tablespoon sesame seeds
- a few sprigs of coriander

Separate the drumsticks from the thighs and season with salt and pepper.

Heat the oil over a medium heat in a wide 25cm/3.2-litre casserole and add the onion, garlic and spices. Cook for a minute or two, stirring, and then add the tomatoes and chicken pieces. Cover and cook gently, stirring occasionally, for about 1¼ hours until the chicken is meltingly tender.

Remove the chicken from the pan and set aside. Return the tomato sauce to the hob and simmer gently, uncovered, for about 20 minutes until the sauce thickens – it should be concentrated and unctuous. The colour will darken somewhat. Stir regularly to prevent the sauce from sticking to the bottom of the pan as the sugar in the tomatoes begins to caramelise. Add the honey. Return the chicken to the casserole to heat through.

Remove the chicken with a slotted spoon to a hot serving dish, spoon over the sauce and garnish with the toasted almonds, sesame seeds and sprigs of fresh coriander.

Everyone loves this spicy dish originally from Sichuan, known as Gong bao or Kung Po, but often better recognised by its American name 'kung pao chicken'. It can be super hot or a little less punchy, depending on the chillies, but don't dumb it down too much as the rice will absorb some of the heat.

Kung pao chicken

- 1 tablespoon cornflour
- 4 tablespoons light soy sauce
- 450g organic, free-range chicken breast or thigh meat, cut into 2.5cm cubes
- 3 tablespoons Shaoxing rice wine
- 2 tablespoons granulated sugar
- 3 tablespoons homemade chicken stock
- 4 teaspoons Chinkiang rice vinegar
- 1 tablespoon sesame oil
- 2 teaspoons dark soy sauce
- 3 tablespoons groundnut or sunflower oil

- 4–12 dried hot red chillies, halved crossways and deseeded
- 5 spring onions (both white and green parts), sliced on the diagonal
- 1 large garlic clove, thinly sliced
- 1cm piece of fresh ginger, grated
- 75g shelled peanuts
- fresh coriander leaves
- 400g boiled basmati rice, to serve

- 340g streaky bacon
- 1 x 1.6kg organic, free-range chicken (or 6 chicken thighs)
- a little extra virgin olive oil, for frying
- 450g baby onions, peeled and left whole
- 340g carrots, peeled and thickly sliced (or left whole if they are small)
- 750ml homemade chicken stock
- a sprig of fresh thyme
- flaky salt and freshly ground black pepper
- 2 tablespoons chopped flat-leaf parsley, to serve

FOR THE HERB CRUST
- 225g plain white flour
- ½ level teaspoon granulated sugar
- ½ level teaspoon bicarbonate of soda
- ½ level teaspoon sea salt
- 1–2 tablespoons chopped mixed herbs, such as rosemary or sage and thyme, chives, flat-leaf parsley or lemon balm
- approx. 175–210ml soured milk or buttermilk, to mix
- a little egg wash, made by beating 1 small organic, free-range egg with a pinch of salt, to glaze
- approx. 50g grated Cheddar cheese (optional)

Mix the cornflour with 1 tablespoon of the light soy sauce in a medium bowl. Add the chicken cubes, toss well to coat and set aside to marinate for about 30 minutes.

Meanwhile, in a small bowl mix together the remaining light soy sauce, rice wine, sugar, chicken stock, vinegar, sesame oil and dark soy sauce.

Heat the oil in a 30–35cm wok or large frying pan over a high heat until just beginning to smoke. Add the chillies, half the spring onions, the garlic, ginger and marinated chicken and stir-fry for 3–5 minutes until the chicken is golden. Add the soy sauce mixture and stir-fry for a further 2–3 minutes until the sauce begins to thicken. Stir in the peanuts. Scatter with the remaining spring onions and lots of coriander, and serve with the basmati rice, if you wish.

SERVES 6

A good chicken casserole may sound a bit passé, but it always gets a hearty welcome from my family and friends. Sometimes I make an entire meal in a pot by covering the top with whole peeled potatoes just before it goes into the oven. If you don't have enough time to sauté the bacon and vegetables, just pop everything into the casserole, cover with chicken stock and season well before you put it into the oven. This is a brilliant family meal with something for everyone in the pot: a 7- or 8-month-old baby starting on solid foods could have a little mashed potato and carrot with some of the rich juice; a little toddler will enjoy sucking on the bones and eating some of the larger pieces of vegetable and potato; and parents can enjoy the entire meal. No need for separate meals for children and adults with this one.

Super-easy chicken casserole *with a herb crust*

Preheat the oven to 180°C/gas mark 4.

Remove the rind from the bacon and cut into 2cm cubes. Joint the chicken into 8 pieces and season well with salt and pepper.

Heat a little oil in a large, ovenproof casserole over a medium heat and cook the bacon until crisp. Remove from the casserole and set aside. Add the chicken pieces to the casserole, a few at a time, and sauté until golden. Heat control is crucial here: the pan mustn't burn, yet it must be hot enough to sauté the chicken. If it is too cool, the chicken pieces will stew rather than sauté and as a result the meat may be tough. Once the chicken pieces are browned, remove from the casserole.

Toss the onions and carrots into the casserole, add a knob of butter and cook for 1–2 minutes until coated. Return the meat to the casserole and pour in the stock. Season well with salt and pepper and pop in a sprig of thyme. Bring up to the boil, then cover with a lid. Transfer the casserole to the oven to cook for an initial 30 minutes while you make the herb crust.

To make the crust, sift the dry ingredients into a large bowl and add the freshly chopped herbs. Make a well in the centre and pour in most of the milk, reserving some for later. Using one hand, gradually bring in the flour from the sides of the bowl and mix to a softish but not too wet and sticky dough, adding more milk if necessary. Turn out onto a floured board, tidy the edges and flip over. Roll the dough to a thickness of 2cm and stamp into rounds with a 5cm cutter.

Once the casserole has cooked for 30 minutes, remove the lid and cover the surface of the stew with slightly overlapping herb scones. Brush with egg wash and sprinkle with a little cheese, if you wish. Increase the heat to 230°C/gas mark 8 and return to the oven for a further 10 minutes. Then reduce the heat to 200°C/gas mark 6 for a final 20 minutes or until the crust is baked and the chicken is cooked through.

Serve bubbling hot, sprinkled with some freshly chopped parsley.

Crisp duck legs, melting onions and potatoes infused with thyme and duck juices – this is definitely one of my favourite winter suppers and it's brilliant for entertaining. Serve with a salad of winter leaves.

Duck legs *with potatoes, onions & thyme leaves*

- 4 organic, free-range duck legs
- extra virgin olive oil, for frying
- 1kg potatoes, peeled and cut into 4cm chunks
- 1kg medium onions, quartered or 450g white turnips, peeled and cut into chunks
- 2 teaspoons thyme leaves
- flaky sea salt and freshly ground black pepper
- sprigs of fresh thyme, to serve

Preheat the oven to 250°C/gas mark 9.

Season the duck legs all over with the salt. Heat a tiny drop of oil in a heavy 25cm/3.2-litre casserole and cook the duck, skin-side down, over a medium heat until well browned. Turn and brown on the other side.

Remove the duck legs to a plate, increase the heat and fry the potatoes and onions in batches until lightly golden, pouring off some of the fat if there is an excessive amount. Sprinkle generously with the thyme leaves and season well with salt and pepper.

Arrange the duck legs on top of the potatoes and onions, cover with a lid and cook in the oven for about 1 hour or until the duck is cooked through and crisp, and the potatoes and onions are soft, juicy and slightly caramelised. Check every now and then.

Serve the duck legs with the potatoes and onions along with the cooking juices, garnished with sprigs of fresh thyme.

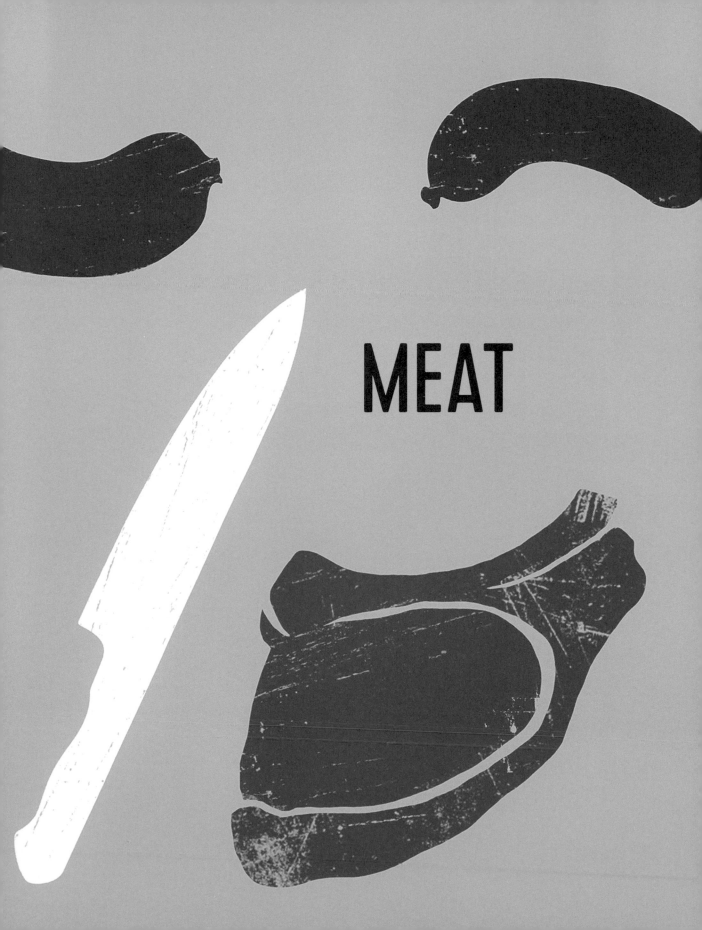

MEAT

The 'eat less meat but better quality' message is really getting through. I love to serve slivers of beautiful, well-hung steak, over a salad of leaves. Here the Crozier Blue crumbles add an irresistible salty note, a whole meal on a platter.

Chargrilled steak & *Crozier Blue salad*

- 2 well-hung sirloin steaks
- 1 large garlic clove, halved
- 1 tablespoon extra virgin olive oil, plus extra for drizzling
- ¼ teaspoon smoked paprika
- a pinch of cayenne pepper
- flaky sea salt and freshly ground black pepper and a little sugar

FOR THE SALAD
- 12-15 ripe red and yellow cherry tomatoes
- 6 radishes
- 4 spring onions, plus extra to garnish
- 1-2 Little Gem lettuce, cut into quarters or sixths
- ⅓–½ cucumber, halved lengthways and sliced at an angle
- society garlic (*Tulbaghia violacea*) or chive blossoms, if available

FOR THE BLUE CHEESE DRESSING
- 100g Crozier Blue or dolcelatte
- 200g soured cream or buttermilk
- 2 tablespoons white wine vinegar
- 4 tablespoons double cream
- ½ teaspoon Dijon mustard
- 1-2 teaspoons honey

Score the fat of the steaks. Rub the surface of the steaks with the cut clove of garlic, then crush the garlic and mix with the extra virgin olive oil, smoked paprika, cayenne pepper, flaky salt and pepper. Dip both sides of the steaks into the spicy oil and allow to soak up the flavours while you make the blue cheese dressing.

To make the dressing, crumble the cheese into the cream (or buttermilk), stir in the wine vinegar, Dijon mustard and honey. Season to taste.

Heat a grill pan over a high heat. Sear the steaks on both sides and continue to cook for 2–4 minutes on each side until medium rare. Turn onto the fat side and cook until it becomes crisp and delicious. You may have to hold it with tongs. Leave the steaks to rest while you prepare the salad.

Slice the tomatoes in half around the equator and others in quarters. Add to a bowl and season with salt and pepper and a little sugar. Slice or quarter the radishes, slice the spring onions lengthways at an angle, add to the bowl, along with the cucumber. Drizzle with a little olive oil and toss. Arrange some of the outer leaves of the Little Gem on a plate, scatter the salad evenly over the platter.

Slice the steak into 5mm thick slices, tuck into the salad. Put a dollop of blue cheese dressing here and there or serve in a separate bowl on the side.

Sprinkle with sliced spring onions and garnish with society garlic flowers or chive blossom, if available. Serve soon.

- 2 tablespoons extra virgin olive oil
- 500–725g stewing meat (beef, veal, mutton or pork), cut into 1–2cm cubes
- 225g onions, chopped
- 2–3 garlic cloves, crushed
- 1 green pepper, deseeded and sliced
- 300ml homemade beef stock or water
- 1 tablespoon tomato purée
- 1 teaspoon ground cumin
- 250g red kidney beans, cooked
- flaky sea salt and brown sugar

FOR THE COLORADO SAUCE
- 6–7 small dried chillies or 4–5 large fresh ones
- 1 large red pepper, deseeded
- 1 large onion, chopped
- 1 large garlic clove, peeled
- sea salt
- 1 tablespoon chipotle chilli in adobo sauce (optional)

FOR THE GUACAMOLE
- 1 ripe avocado (Hass if available)
- 1–2 tablespoons freshly squeezed lime juice
- 1 tablespoon extra virgin olive oil
- 1 tablespoon chopped coriander or flat-leaf parsley
- freshly ground black pepper

FOR THE TOMATO & CORIANDER SALSA
- 4 very ripe tomatoes, chopped
- 1 tablespoon chopped red or white onion
- 1 garlic clove, crushed
- ½–1 red or green chilli, such as Jalapeño or Serrano, deseeded and finely chopped
- 1–2 tablespoons chopped coriander
- a squeeze of organic lime juice
- flaky sea salt, freshly ground black pepper and sugar

TO SERVE
- 125g soured cream
- 125g Cheddar cheese, grated
- a generous handful of fresh coriander leaves
- 36–40 tortilla chips

SERVES 6

Buy stewing meat for this dish, rather than the finest cuts, and try to avoid minced beef. Colorado sauce is a delicious sauce to use when making chilli con carne, rather than chilli powder. It is very versatile and can also be used as a marinade for grilled or barbecued meats.

Chilli *con carne*

Start with the Colorado sauce. If the chillies are dried, soak them in a little water for an hour, then slit them and wash out the seeds. Discard the stalks and do the same with the red pepper. Purée all the sauce ingredients in a food processor, adding a little of the chilli soaking water if necessary. If you are using fresh chillies, you might need to add a tablespoon or two of cold water. Season to taste with salt. Add the chilli in adobo sauce, if using.

Heat a splash of extra virgin olive oil in a large casserole over a high heat and brown the meat in batches. Remove to a plate. Add the onion, reduce the heat to medium and fry for 4-5 minutes until soft and just beginning to colour. Add the crushed garlic and continue to cook for a minute or two. Return the meat to the pan and add the green pepper and Colorado sauce. Pour in just enough stock or water to barely cover the ingredients. Cover the pan tightly with a lid and simmer gently over a low heat for about 30 minutes, or until the meat is cooked and the sauce has reduced to a thick, brownish-red sauce. Check the liquid occasionally and if it seems to be reducing too quickly reduce the heat further and top up with water.

Add the tomato purée, cumin and cooked kidney beans. Season with salt and brown sugar. Simmer for a further 15 minutes.

Meanwhile, make the guacamole. Scoop out the flesh from the avocado and mash it with a fork. Add the lime juice, olive oil and chopped coriander or parsley, and season to taste with black pepper. If you are not serving immediately, cover the surface with a layer of clingfilm and chill until needed.

To make the tomato and coriander salsa, mix all of the ingredients together and season to taste with salt, pepper and sugar.

To serve, put a blob of soured cream on top of the chilli, sprinkle with the grated cheese and garnish with some fresh coriander. Accompany with the tortilla chips, guacamole and tomato salsa.

This is super tasty, so a little goes a long way — but it's so worth using fresh lime leaves. Lime trees are now available to purchase from good garden centres. I have several plants at home in large pots, which are becoming quite shrubby — the leaves freeze pretty well and make a brilliant gift for a friend who loves to cook.

Thai beef curry *with peanut sauce*

- 600ml coconut milk
- 15–45ml red curry paste
- 45ml fish sauce
- 2½ tablespoons palm sugar or soft brown sugar
- 2 stalks of fresh lemongrass, bruised
- 450g rump steak, cut into thin strips
- 75g roasted peanuts, finely chopped or pulsed in a food processor
- 1–2 red chillies, sliced
- 5 kaffir lime leaves, torn – fresh are best, but otherwise use dried
- flaky sea salt and freshly ground black pepper
- 10–15 Thai basil leaves (optional)

FOR THE THAI JASMINE RICE
- 340g Thai jasmine rice
- 340ml water

Start by cooking the sticky rice. Put the rice and water into a heavy-based saucepan and bring to the boil. Stir once, cover with a tight-fitting lid (if your lid isn't tight fitting, cover the pan first with parchment and then with the lid). Reduce the heat to the absolute minimum – use a heat diffuser mat, if you have one. Cook on the lowest possible heat for 15 minutes. Do not uncover during cooking. Remove the pan from the heat, keeping it covered, and set aside for 5 minutes before serving. The rice will stay warm for several hours if necessary.

To make the curry, pour half the coconut milk into a wok and cook over a medium heat, stirring, until the milk boils and separates – it will look curdled, but don't worry. Whisk in the red curry paste and cook for 3–4 minutes until fragrant and aromatic. Add the fish sauce, palm sugar or brown sugar and lemongrass. Continue to cook over a gentle heat for a few minutes before adding the rest of the coconut milk. Bring back to the boil.

Add the strips of beef and the peanuts, stir and cook gently for 6–7 minutes or until most of the liquid has evaporated. Be careful not to overcook the beef. If necessary, you can remove the meat with a slotted spoon after the allotted cooking time and return the pan to the heat to reduce the sauce further. Return the meat to the pan, if necessary, and throw in the chillies and lime leaves. Season to taste and remove the lemongrass.

Serve with the Thai fragrant rice, garnished with Thai basil leaves, if available.

This is a rich and delicious stew that just gets better and better. The flavour deepens when made the day before. Serve with polenta, tagliatelle or some fluffy mashed potato and a tasty green salad, as you wish.

Beef & Agen prune stew

- 18 Agen mi-cuit or semi-soft prunes, stoned
- 2 tablespoons extra virgin olive oil
- 400g carrots, cut into 1cm slices
- 285g onions, sliced
- 1.35kg well-hung stewing beef or lean flank, trimmed of fat and cut into 4cm cubes
- 1 heaped tablespoon plain flour
- 150ml red wine
- 150ml brown beef stock
- 1 x 400g tin of chopped tomatoes
- 8 medium potatoes, washed and peeled at the last minute
- 2 tablespoons chopped flat-leaf parsley
- flaky sea salt and freshly ground black pepper
- a good green salad and some polenta, tagliatelle or mashed potatoes, to serve (optional)

Preheat the oven to 160°C/gas mark 3.

Place the prunes in a bowl, cover with boiling water and set aside to soak.

Heat 1 tablespoon olive oil in a 25cm/3.2-litre casserole over a gentle heat and cook the sliced carrots and onions for 10 minutes, covered, until soft. Remove from the pan and set aside on a plate.

Heat another tablespoon of olive oil in the casserole over a medium heat until almost smoking. Add the pieces of beef and sear on all sides in the hot fat. Reduce the heat to low, stir in the flour and cook for 1 minute. Pour in the wine, stock and chopped tomatoes and bring slowly to the boil, stirring. Add the onions and carrots back to the pan and season with salt and pepper. Cover with a lid and simmer gently for 1¼ hours.

Arrange the whole peeled potatoes on top of the meat and vegetables and replace the lid. Return the casserole to the oven and continue to cook for a further 1 hour or until the meat is tender. Add the whole drained prunes and chopped parsley about 15 minutes before the end.

Serve with a green salad and some tagliatelle, polenta or mashed potatoes, if you like.

The word tagine refers both to the distinctive earthenware cooking pot with its shallow base and conical top and to the multitude of stew-like dishes that are cooked in it. These can be based on meat, fish, poultry or vegetables. In Morocco, tagine is eaten alone but I am including a recipe for plain couscous in case you'd enjoy it as an accompaniment.

Tagine of lamb *with preserved lemon*

- 1.35kg boned shoulder of lamb, trimmed of fat and cut into 4cm cubes
- scant 2 teaspoons ground cinnamon
- 1 teaspoon ground ginger
- 1 teaspoon freshly ground black pepper
- a generous pinch of saffron threads
- 175g raisins
- 50g butter
- 2 onions, chopped
- 2 garlic cloves, finely chopped
- salt
- 2 tablespoons honey
- 3 tablespoons chopped coriander
- 1 small or ½ large preserved lemon, diced
- 50g toasted flaked almonds

FOR THE COUSCOUS
- 350g couscous
- 450ml boiling water
- 4 tablespoons extra virgin olive oil
- flaky sea salt and freshly ground black pepper

TO SERVE
- coriander sprigs and chopped mint (optional)
- natural yogurt

Combine the cinnamon, ginger, black pepper and saffron with 4 tablespoons of water in a large bowl. Add the lamb and toss well to coat. If you have the time, you can marinate the lamb for up to 24 hours, covered, in the fridge. Place the raisins in a bowl, cover with water and set aside to plump up while you cook the lamb.

Melt the butter in a tagine or a large heavy-based frying pan with a lid. Add the lamb, onions, garlic, ½ teaspoon of salt and enough water to come halfway up the meat. Bring up to the boil, cover the pan with a lid and reduce the heat to a gentle simmer. Cook for about an hour, turning the lamb occasionally until the meat is meltingly tender.

Add the drained raisins, honey and half the fresh coriander. Continue to cook for a further 30 minutes or so over a gentle heat, uncovered, until the sauce is thick and unctuous. Season to taste.

While the tagine is cooking, scoop out the flesh from the preserved lemon and discard, then chop up the peel.

To make the couscous, put the couscous into a Pyrex bowl. Pour over the boiling water from the kettle, cover with the bowl with clingfilm and set aside to soak for 15 minutes. Stir with a fork to break up the clumps, mix in the olive oil and season with salt and pepper.

Sprinkle the preserved lemon, almonds and the remaining coriander over the lamb just before serving. Natural yogurt makes a delicious accompaniment. I also love to stir in some freshly chopped mint. There's no need to serve with any vegetables, but a green salad would be a delicious addition.

Bean stews make the perfect one-pot meal — comforting, filling and inexpensive. Gremolata is a fresh-tasting mix of chopped parsley, garlic and lemon zest. I use it to sprinkle over roast or braised meats, pastas or anything pan-grilled — delicious! If you're short of time, you could replace it with some chopped parsley instead.

Slow-cooked lamb *with cannellini beans, tomatoes & rosemary*

- 500g boned leg or shoulder of lamb, trimmed of fat and cut into 3cm cubes
- plain flour, for dusting
- 2 tablespoons extra virgin olive oil
- 50g onions, finely chopped
- 2 garlic cloves, finely chopped
- 225g carrots, finely diced
- 1 stick of celery, finely diced
- 2 bay leaves
- a few generous sprigs of rosemary
- 2 x 400g tins of Italian chopped tomatoes
- 350ml white wine
- 350ml homemade lamb stock or water
- 2 x 400g tins of cannellini beans, rinsed in cold water and drained
- flaky sea salt and freshly ground black pepper

FOR THE GREMOLATA
- 4 tablespoons chopped flat-leaf parsley
- 1 generous teaspoon grated or finely chopped organic lemon zest
- 2 garlic cloves, finely chopped
- flaky sea salt, to taste

Dust the cubes of lamb with flour and season with salt and pepper. Heat the olive oil in a casserole and fry the lamb in batches until brown. Remove the lamb to a plate and set aside.

Add the onions, garlic, carrots and celery to the casserole and cook over a medium heat for 3–4 minutes until the onions are beginning to soften and are slightly golden. Add the lamb.

Reduce the heat to low and put in the bay leaves, rosemary, tomatoes, white wine and lamb stock or water. Bring slowly to the boil, cover the pan with a lid and simmer very gently for about 1½ hours, or until the lamb is tender. Add the cannellini beans 15 minutes before the end.

To make the gremolata, mix all of the ingredients in a small bowl, season to taste with salt and serve soon.

Remove the rosemary sprigs from the lamb and check the seasoning. Serve with the gremolata.

This rich spicy dish is often better reheated the next day, or the day after. If you have any of the sauce left over, toss it with some pasta or noodles for a simple supper.

Masala lamb shanks

- 8 lamb shanks, weighing approx. 1.2kg in total
- 1 tablespoon ground turmeric
- 3cm piece of fresh ginger, grated
- 3 garlic cloves, crushed
- 2 tablespoons extra virgin olive oil
- 1 bay leaf
- 1 cinnamon stick
- 5 cloves
- 6 cardamom pods, bashed
- 450g onions, sliced
- 1 x 400g tin of chopped tomatoes
- 1–2 teaspoons honey
- 2 teaspoons ground cumin
- 3 teaspoons ground coriander
- 2–3 green chillies, halved
- 1 x 400ml tin of coconut milk
- 8 large potatoes, peeled and halved
- sea salt
- lots of fresh coriander sprigs, to serve

FOR THE MASALA PASTE
- 25g desiccated coconut
- 1½ tablespoons coriander seeds
- 1 tablespoon poppy seeds
- 1 tablespoon fennel seeds
- 1 tablespoon mustard seeds
- ½ tablespoon freshly ground black pepper
- 2–3 red chillies, finely chopped

FOR THE MINT YOGURT
- 4 tablespoons chopped mint
- 300ml natural yogurt
- sea salt and a little honey, to taste

Put the lamb shanks into a 27-29cm/4.1-4.7-litre casserole and add the turmeric, ginger, garlic and some salt. Pour in enough water to cover (approx. 2.4 litres) and bring slowly to the boil. Reduce the heat, cover with a lid, and simmer gently for 2 hours or until the meat is tender.

Meanwhile, grind the ingredients for the masala paste in a spice grinder or pestle and mortar, and set aside until needed.

Once the lamb shanks are cooked, remove them carefully from the pan and keep warm. Pour all of the cooking liquid into a separate pan and set aside.

Return the casserole to a low heat with the extra virgin olive oil. Add the bay leaf, cinnamon, cloves and cardamom and stir-fry for 1–2 minutes. Add the onions and fry for 5-6 minutes until they start to soften. Add the chopped tomatoes and honey and cook for 5 minutes. Sprinkle in the ground cumin and coriander, add the green chillies and cook for 3 minutes. Finally stir in the masala paste and coconut milk and bring slowly to the boil. Taste and add salt, if necessary.

Return the cooked lamb shanks to the pan and pour in enough of the cooking liquid to come halfway up the shanks. Bring to the boil, cover with a lid and simmer gently for 10 minutes, turning the shanks several times during the cooking time.

Add the potatoes to the pan, replace the lid and cook for 20 minutes or until the potatoes are fully cooked and the lamb is almost falling off the bone. Season to taste.

To make the mint yogurt, stir the chopped mint into the yogurt and season to taste with salt and honey.

Sprinkle the casserole with lots of fresh coriander and serve with the mint yogurt.

A substantial pot of stew fortified with pearl barley,
this is really good with lots of gremolata sprinkled
over the top. It is a variation of Irish stew, which is the
quintessential one-pot dish – the recipe for the original
Ballymaloe version can be found in my *Forgotten Skills
of Cooking* book.

Lamb & pearl barley
stew & *fresh herb gremolata*

- 350g piece of green streaky bacon
  (blanched if salty)
- 1.8kg gigot or rack chops from the
  shoulder of lamb, not less than
  2.5cm thick
- well-seasoned plain flour,
  for dusting
- a little extra virgin olive oil,
  for frying
- 350g mushrooms, thinly sliced
- 700g whole, small onions – baby
  ones are nicest
- 350g carrots, peeled and thickly sliced
- 150g parsnips, peeled and thickly sliced
- 400g pearl barley
- approx. 2.8 litres homemade lamb
  or chicken stock
- sprig of thyme
- flaky sea salt and freshly ground
  black pepper

FOR THE GREMOLATA
- 4 tablespoons chopped mixed herbs,
  such as flat-leaf parsley, chervil and mint
- 2 garlic cloves, finely chopped
- 1 generous teaspoon grated or finely
  chopped organic lemon zest
- flaky sea salt, to taste

Preheat the oven to 180°C/gas mark 4.

First make the stew. Cut the rind off the bacon and cut into
approx. 1cm cubes. Divide the lamb into 8 pieces and roll in
the well-seasoned flour.

Heat a little oil in a 25cm/3.2-litre casserole over a medium
heat and sauté the bacon until crisp. Remove to a plate.
Sauté the mushrooms, season well and set aside. Add the
lamb to the casserole in batches, with a little more olive oil if
necessary, and sauté until golden. Heat control is crucial here:
the pan mustn't burn, yet it must be hot enough to sauté the
lamb. If the pan is too cool, the lamb will stew rather than
sauté and as a result the meat may be tough. Remove the
lamb to a plate. Add another splash of olive oil to the pan and
sauté the onions, carrots and parsnips until golden. Return
the bacon and lamb to the casserole, together with the pearl
barley. Season well, pour in the stock, add the thyme and bring
to a simmer. Cover with a lid and transfer to the oven for 1–1¼
hours until meltingly tender; the cooking time will depend on
the age of the lamb and how long it was sautéed for. Add the
mushrooms about 30 minutes before the end.

Meanwhile, make the gremolata. Mix together the chopped
herbs and garlic in a small bowl, add the lemon zest and
season to taste with a little flaky salt.

Once the casserole is cooked, remove the thyme and season
to taste. Leave the casserole to sit for 15–30 minutes to allow
the pearl barley to swell. (If necessary, the casserole can be
reheated later in the day, or the next day.) Serve bubbling hot,
sprinkled with the gremolata.

SERVES 4-6

This delicious Greek-inspired lamb, squash and orzo stew is tender, rich and sweet – a perfect one-pot winter supper. You can increase the quantity of orzo to 225g if you wish, but I like the proportion as it is.

Lamb, *butternut squash* & *orzo* stew

- 2 tablespoons extra virgin olive oil
- 200g onions, sliced
- 1 x 5–7.5cm cinnamon stick
- 1 tablespoon chopped marjoram
- 2 sprigs of fresh thyme
- 1kg organic boned shoulder of lamb, trimmed of fat and cut into roughly 4cm cubes
- 1 x 400g tin of plum tomatoes, roughly chopped
- 600ml homemade lamb or chicken stock
- 400g butternut squash, peeled and cut into 2.5cm cubes
- 200g orzo
- 2 tablespoons grated Parmesan cheese
- 2 tablespoons chopped flat-leaf parsley
- zest of ½ organic lemon
- flaky sea salt and freshly ground black pepper

FOR THE MINTED YOGURT
- 225ml Greek or thick natural yogurt
- 2 tablespoons chopped mint leaves
- 1 teaspoon freshly squeezed organic lemon juice

Preheat the oven to 160°C/gas mark 3.

Heat the olive oil in a large 24cm 4.2-litre casserole over a medium heat. Add the onions, cinnamon stick, marjoram and thyme and cook for 4-5 minutes until the onions start to soften. Fry the lamb in batches until lightly browned, and then season with plenty of salt and pepper. Add the chopped tomatoes and their juice and pour in about 450ml of the stock. Bring to the boil, and then cover the pan with a lid and transfer to the oven for about 1 hour. Remove the pan from the oven, stir in the squash and season again. Replace the lid and return to the oven for a further 20 minutes. Stir in the orzo and cook on the hob or return to the oven for a further 20 minutes. Degrease if necessary with a spoon.

To make the minted yogurt, mix together the yogurt, mint and lemon juice in a small bowl.

Sprinkle the stew with the Parmesan, chopped parsley and lemon zest and serve immediately with the minted yogurt.

So named because traditionally in France local people would have brought their cassoulet, gratins and roasts to be cooked in the residual heat of the baker's wood-burning oven after he had finished baking the bread – hence the name *à la boulangère*. Nothing could be simpler: slide a roasting tin of boulangère potatoes into the oven, sit a leg of lamb on a rack above and, as the lamb cooks, its delicious juices drip onto the potatoes to enrich the dish further.

Lamb *à la boulangère*

- approx. 3kg organic leg of lamb
- 3kg potatoes
- 50g butter
- 3 large onions, thinly sliced
- 1 tablespoon thyme leaves
- 850ml hot homemade lamb or chicken stock
- flaky sea salt and freshly ground black pepper
- green salad, to serve

Preheat the oven to 180°C/gas mark 4.

Season the leg of lamb with salt and pepper. If it's a big leg, and you suspect it may take longer than an hour to cook, pop it on a rack in the preheated oven while you prepare the potatoes (have a container not far beneath to catch the juices). Prepare the potatoes by peeling them and cutting them into slices about 5mm thick.

Butter a roasting tin approx. 33 x 23cm and arrange the potatoes in alternating layers with the sliced onions and a sprinkling of thyme leaves. Season each layer with salt and pepper. Arrange the top layer of potatoes in overlapping slices. Pour in the hot stock and dot with the remaining butter.

Slide the tin into the oven, right under the rack with the leg of lamb cooking on it so that the juices drip down. Bake for 1–1½ hours or until the potatoes are cooked and the top is golden brown and crusty. Carve the lamb in thick slices and serve with a generous helping of boulangère potatoes and a good green salad.

A shoulder of pork is the best cut to use for this long, slow cooking method, as the meat is layered with fat which slowly melts away. Try to find a traditional breed, such as Gloucester Old Spot, Saddleback, Black Berkshire, Middle White or Mangalitza. Slow-cooked shoulder of pork can be served in so many ways with so many accompaniments, but I love it as a filler for tacos along with all the toppings.

Pork taco *party*

- 1 x 2.75–3.25kg whole shoulder of organic, free-range pork, skin on
- 8 garlic cloves, peeled
- 25g fennel seeds
- flaky sea salt and freshly ground black pepper
- 1 teaspoon chilli flakes (optional)
- 2 teaspoons thyme leaves

TO SERVE
- 16–20 soft corn tortillas - have a few extra on hand depending on how ravenous people are
- guacamole (page 65) or slices of avocado
- tomato salsa (page 65)
- hot sauce
- 6–8 spring onions, cut on the diagonal
- 8–10 tablespoons coriander leaves
- 3 organic limes, halved, for squeezing

Preheat the oven to 180°C/gas mark 4.

Using a small sharp knife or, better still, a Stanley knife, score the rind of the pork with deep cuts about 5mm apart.

Crush the garlic with the fennel seeds in a pestle and mortar and mix in some salt and pepper and a few chilli flakes (if using). Sprinkle over the pork, rubbing it into the cuts, over the rind and all over the surface of the meat.

Place the shoulder of pork on a rack in an approx. 33 x 30cm roasting tin and roast for 30 minutes or until the skin begins to blister and brown. Reduce the temperature to 130°C/gas mark 1 and continue to roast for 5–6 hours until the meat is completely soft under the crisp skin. By this time, the meat should give way and almost fall off the bone. Pour off the delicious pork fat from time to time and save it in jars for roasting or sautéing potatoes another day.

Lift the crisp skin off the slow-cooked pork, chop and keep warm. Lift the pork off the bones and shred into a large serving bowl.

Strain the pork pan juices into a measuring jug and pour off and discard all the fat from the surface. Add the rich juices to the pork. Season the meat with salt and pepper, a few chilli flakes and some thyme leaves. Keep hot.

Lay out the accompaniments on the table: a pile of soft corn tortillas, a bowl of guacamole or sliced avocado, some tomato salsa, a bottle of hot sauce, some slivered spring onions and fresh coriander. Bring the hot meat and crackling to the table and allow everyone to help themselves.

A gorgeous pot of bean stew, so warm and comforting for an autumn or winter supper. Use your favourite juicy heritage pork sausages.

Sausage, haricot or flageolet beans *with tomato & rosemary*

- 225g dried haricot, cannellini or flageolet beans (or 2 x 400g tins of cooked beans)
- bouquet garni
- 1 carrot, peeled
- 1 onion, peeled
- 3 tablespoons extra virgin olive oil, plus extra for frying
- 450g fennel and chilli pork sausages
- 175g chopped onion
- 4 large garlic cloves, crushed
- 1 x 400g tin of plum tomatoes, chopped
- 1 tablespoon chopped rosemary
- flaky sea salt, freshly ground black pepper and sugar
- flat-leaf parsley or chervil, to serve

Variations

CHEESY SAUSAGE, HARICOT OR FLAGEOLET BEANS WITH TOMATO & ROSEMARY

Spoon the finished stew into a shallow ovenproof dish and scatter over 50g breadcrumbs mixed with 25g butter and 50g grated Cheddar cheese. Flash under the grill until crisp and golden on top.

HARICOT OR FLAGEOLET BEANS WITH TOMATO & ROSEMARY WITH CHORIZO OR 'NDUJA

Omit the sausages and add 125g sliced chorizo or pieces of 'nduja to the tomato base with the beans and rosemary.

Soak the beans overnight in a large pan with plenty of cold water. Next day, strain the beans, discarding the soaking liquid, and return them to the pan. Cover with fresh cold water and add the bouquet garni, carrot and onion. Cover the pan with a lid and simmer for 30 minutes–1 hour until the beans are soft, but not mushy. Just before the end of cooking, season with salt. Remove the bouquet garni and vegetables from the pan and discard. Drain the beans, reserving the cooking liquid.

Fry the sausages in a few drops of oil over a medium heat until nicely coloured and remove from the pan and set aside.

Heat the oil over a lowish heat in the same saucepan and cook the chopped onion for 7–8 minutes until soft but not coloured. Add the garlic and cook for a further minute or two before adding the chopped tomatoes and their juice, the cooked beans and the rosemary. Add the sausages and simmer for 5–6 minutes, adding some of the bean liquid if the sauce starts to dry out. Season well with salt, freshly ground black pepper and sugar. Cook for a further 5–6 minutes or until the sausages are heated through. The mixture should be juicy, but not swimming in liquid – if it starts to dry out, add more of the bean liquid.

To serve, scatter with plenty of parsley and accompany with a salad of organic leaves or crusty bread, if you wish.

Another perennial favourite, served here with
orzo – a form of pasta that looks much like grains of
rice. Pork fillet is sometimes referred to as pork steak
or pork tenderloin. Chicken breast works brilliantly
here also and the whole dish reheats perfectly.

Fillet of pork *with mushroom, rosemary & ginger*

- 2 x 500g organic, free-range pork fillets
- 30g butter
- 1 teaspoon chopped rosemary
- 2 tablespoons chopped shallot or
  spring onion
- 110g autumn chanterelle mushrooms,
  roughly chopped (or thinly sliced
  flat mushrooms if chanterelles are
  not available)
- 600ml homemade chicken stock
- 1–2 teaspoons grated fresh ginger
- 150ml double cream
- 200g orzo
- flaky sea salt and freshly ground
  black pepper
- sprigs of fresh rosemary and rosemary
  flowers if in season, to garnish

Trim the pork fillet of all fat and membrane. Cut into slices 2cm thick.

Heat half of the butter in a 22cm sauté pan until foaming, put in the pork and turn in the butter – do not let it brown. Add the chopped rosemary and toss to coat. Cover the pan with a round of greaseproof paper and the lid, and cook over a gentle heat for 5–7 minutes or until the pork is barely cooked. Remove the meat and juices to a plate.

Melt the remaining butter in the same pan over a lowish heat and sweat the shallots very gently for 4–5 minutes until soft. Increase the heat, add the mushrooms and season with salt and pepper. Cook for 3–4 minutes until limp and fully cooked, and then remove the mushrooms to the plate with the pork (be careful not to overcook, or the lean pork will be dry).

Pour the chicken stock into the pan and add the ginger and cream. Bring to the boil, add ½ teaspoon of salt and stir in the orzo. Cover the pan with a lid and cook for 8 minutes with the lid on, and then 2 minutes with the lid off.

Add the pork and mushrooms back to the pan, adjust the seasoning and heat through for 2 minutes. Serve immediately, garnished with the fresh rosemary.

Based on a simple batter, this savoury equivalent of the French dessert clafoutis can be whipped up in minutes. Here I use regular sausages, but I also love to use spicy varieties, such as merguez or chorizo. A little grainy mustard adds extra oomph.

Toad in the hole *with lots of fresh herbs*

- 450g homemade sausages or spicy sausages, such as merguez or chorizo
- 1–2 tablespoons extra virgin olive oil
- 1–2 tablespoons coarsely chopped flat-leaf parsley, to serve

FOR THE BATTER
- 225g plain white flour
- 4 organic, free-range eggs
- 600ml whole milk
- 30g butter, melted
- 1 teaspoon Dijon mustard (optional)
- 4 tablespoons mixed chopped herbs, such as flat-leaf parsley, thyme, chives and marjoram
- ½–1 teaspoon flaky sea salt and plenty of freshly ground black pepper

Preheat the oven to 230°C/gas mark 8.

To make the batter, sift the flour into a bowl, make a well in the centre and crack in the lightly beaten eggs. Using a small whisk or wooden spoon and stirring continuously, gradually draw in the flour from the sides, adding the milk in a steady stream at the same time. Once all the flour has been incorporated, whisk in the remaining milk and the cooled melted butter, along with the mustard (if using) and the herbs. Season with salt and pepper. Set aside to rest while you cook the sausages.

Heat a little extra virgin olive oil in a 23 x 40cm roasting tin, 4cm deep, add the sausages, cook until golden on all sides.

Pour the batter over the sausages and bake for 20–25 minutes until the batter is well risen and crisp. Sprinkle with chopped fresh parsley and serve.

Variation

TOAD IN THE HOLE WITH JAM & CREAM
For a quick sweet bite, make the batter as above, cook in individual patty tins or muffin tins. Serve with a blob of jam and softly whipped cream in the centre. Dust with icing sugar, to serve.

The flavour of this stew really improves if you cook it the day before and reheat it the next day – as well as improving the flavour, cooking the venison in advance ensures that it is meltingly tender. If 'needs must' and you are racing against the clock, just mix all the ingredients in the casserole, bring to the boil and simmer until cooked. Baked potatoes work brilliantly with venison stew, but a layer of potatoes on top provides a wonderfully comforting meal in one pot. Scatter lots of fresh parsley over the potatoes before tucking in.

Venison & parsnip stew

- 1.3kg shoulder of venison, trimmed and cut into 4cm cubes
- 50g plain flour, for dusting
- 2 tablespoons extra virgin olive oil
- 225g piece of fatty salted pork or green streaky bacon, cut into 4cm cubes
- 2 large onions, chopped
- 1 large carrot, diced
- 2 large parsnips, diced
- 1 large garlic clove, crushed
- 450ml homemade beef stock
- bouquet garni
- 8–12 medium potatoes
- a squeeze of organic lemon juice
- flaky sea salt and freshly ground black pepper

FOR THE MARINADE
- 300–350ml gutsy red wine
- 1 medium onion, sliced
- 3 tablespoons brandy
- 3 tablespoons extra virgin olive oil
- bouquet garni
- horseradish sauce (optional)

TO SERVE
- lots of chopped flat-leaf parsley
- green vegetables, such as Brussels sprouts, calabrese or cabbage

First marinate the meat. Season the cubes of venison with salt and pepper. Combine all of the ingredients for the marinade in a large bowl, add the venison and set aside to marinate for at least 1 hour, or better still overnight.

Preheat the oven to 150°C/gas mark 2.

Drain the meat, reserving the marinade, and pat dry with kitchen paper. Tip the flour onto a plate and season well. Turn the cubes of venison in the seasoned flour to coat on all sides.

Heat the oil in a 25cm/3.2-litre casserole pan over a low heat, add the salted pork or bacon and cook for 4–5 minutes, stirring, until it starts to release its fat. Increase the heat to medium and fry the salted pork or bacon until golden brown. Transfer to a plate and set aside.

Add the venison to the casserole in batches and fry over a medium heat until nicely coloured on all sides. Avoid the temptation to increase the temperature or the fat will burn. Remove and set the batch aside while you colour the rest.

Toss the vegetables in the casserole, stir in the garlic and then add the pork or bacon and venison.

Pour off any surplus fat from the casserole and remove the meat and veg and set aside. Deglaze the casserole by pouring in the strained marinade. Bring to the boil, stirring to dissolve the crusty bits on the base, add the pork or bacon and vegetables back in. →

Pour over enough stock to cover the meat and vegetables, and put in the bouquet garni. Bring the casserole to a gentle simmer on the hob, then cover with a lid and transfer to the oven for 1½ hours.

Remove the casserole from the oven and cover the surface of the stew with the whole potatoes. Season with salt and pepper. Cover the potatoes with a circle of greaseproof paper, and then the lid. Return the casserole to the oven and cook for a further 1 hour or until both the venison and potatoes are cooked.

Season to taste. As well as adding salt and pepper, I find it often needs a bit of acidity in the form of lemon juice or crab apple jelly, if available.

Scatter with lots of freshly chopped parsley and serve with a nice big dish of Brussels sprouts, calabrese or cabbage and some homemade horseradish sauce.

I love this combination, in fact I'm rather addicted to the Irish smoked black pudding made in the traditional way with fresh blood and natural casings. The texture is soft and crumbly and totally delicious.

Smoked black pudding *with charred onions & Jerusalem artichokes*

- 4 medium onions, peeled
- extra virgin olive oil, for drizzling
- 6–8 medium Jerusalem artichokes, scrubbed really well
- 200g piece of smoked black pudding or traditional black pudding, skin removed and cut into 16 pieces
- 8 sprigs of watercress
- 1 teaspoon Forum Chardonnay vinegar or good-quality white wine vinegar
- flaky sea salt and freshly ground black pepper

FOR THE APPLE & HORSERADISH SAUCE
- 300ml apple sauce
- 125ml double cream
- 2–3 rounded teaspoons grated fresh horseradish

Preheat the oven to 250°C/gas mark 9.

Halve the onions and brush the cut side with extra virgin olive oil. Season with salt and pepper, and arrange on an approx. 40 x 43cm roasting tray lined with parchment paper.

Slice the artichokes into 7mm rounds and place in a bowl. Drizzle over 1 tablespoon olive oil, season well with salt and pepper and arrange in a single layer around the onions.

Roast for 30–35 minutes until the vegetables are cooked and well coloured.

Place the pieces of black pudding in the same bowl, drizzle over 2 teaspoons of olive oil and toss well to coat. Arrange the black pudding over the roasted vegetables and roast for a further 3–4 minutes until coloured.

To make the sauce, combine the apple sauce and cream in a small pan, bring to the boil and stir in the horseradish.

Place the sprigs of watercress in a bowl and drizzle with the vinegar and 3 teaspoons of extra virgin olive oil. Toss well to coat.

To serve, divide the dressed watercress between eight plates and arrange half an onion and two pieces of black pudding on each. Scatter with the artichokes and dollop the sauce here and there.

FISH + SEAFOOD

Pronounced 'poh-kay', this Hawaiian version of sashimi or ceviche is often made with really fresh raw tuna. Raw mackerel is also delicious.

Mackerel poke

- 8 super-fresh mackerel fillets or 800g fresh tuna, cut into 2cm chunks
- 1 small cucumber, cut into 1cm dice
- 2 avocados, stoned, peeled and cut into 2.5cm cubes
- 8 spring onions, sliced on the diagonal
- 1 tablespoon each of toasted black and white sesame seeds
- 1-2 sheets of nori, snipped into strips
- coriander leaves, to garnish

FOR THE SUSHI RICE
- 450g sushi rice 'No 1 Extra Fancy'
- 600ml water

FOR THE VINEGAR WATER
- 50ml rice wine vinegar
- 1½ tablespoons granulated sugar
- 2½ teaspoons salt

FOR THE MIRIN DRESSING
- 2 tablespoons rice wine vinegar
- 4 teaspoons sesame oil
- 1 tablespoon mirin
- 2 tablespoons soy sauce
- juice of 2 organic limes

First prepare the sushi rice. Rinse the rice for 10 minutes in a colander or sieve under cold running water or until the water becomes clear. Tip the rice into a heavy-based saucepan, cover with 600ml cold water and set aside for 30–45 minutes to 'wake up the rice'.

Bring the rice to the boil and simmer for 10 minutes until all of the water has been absorbed. Avoid the temptation to stir the rice or remove the lid. Increase the heat right at the end for the last 10 seconds, just before you turn off the heat. Remove the lid, place a tea towel over the rice and replace the lid. Set aside for 20 minutes.

To make the vinegar water, combine the rice wine vinegar, sugar and salt in a medium bowl and stir until the sugar and salt have dissolved. Scoop out the rice into a flat timber or earthenware bowl. While the rice is still hot, pour the vinegar solution over the rice and mix together in a slicing action with the aid of a straight-ended wooden spoon. Do not stir. You must do this quickly, preferably cooling the rice with a fan – which is much easier to do if you have a helper. Leave the rice to cool, covered with kitchen paper or a tea towel to soak up any excess moisture as it cools.

To make the mirin dressing, whisk the rice wine vinegar, sesame oil, mirin, soy sauce and freshly squeezed lime juice in a medium bowl. Add the mackerel (or tuna) and turn in the dressing. Add the diced cucumber and cubed avocado and toss gently together.

Divide the cooled rice between shallow bowls and top with the mackerel mixture. Sprinkle with the spring onions, sesame seeds and some shards of nori, and garnish with fresh coriander leaves. Drizzle any remaining dressing over the top and serve right away.

There are always gasps of appreciation when I bring a pot of this fish stew to the table. If you don't have Serrano ham, use a little diced chorizo or 'nduja. Provide lots of crusty sourdough to mop up all the juices.

Andalusian shellfish stew

- ½ teaspoon saffron strands
- 600ml homemade chicken stock
- approx. 6 tablespoons extra virgin olive oil
- 2 onions, chopped
- 2 garlic cloves, crushed
- 1 large red pepper, deseeded and sliced
- 1 large green pepper, deseeded and sliced
- 6–12 waxy potatoes, cut into 2.5cm dice
- 110g piece of Serrano ham, cut into 1cm dice
- 1 x 400g tin of butter beans or cannellini beans *
- 1.8kg cockles or mussels, or a mixture, scrubbed and washed really well
- flaky sea salt and freshly ground black pepper

TO SERVE
- 4–6 ripe tomatoes, peeled and very finely chopped
- sprigs of flat-leaf parsley

Put the saffron into a little bowl and cover with 2–3 tablespoons of chicken stock. Set aside to infuse.

Heat the olive oil in a 25cm sauté pan over a gentle heat and sweat the onions and garlic for 4–5 minutes until soft and slightly coloured. Add the sliced peppers, season with salt and pepper and continue to cook over a medium heat for 6–8 minutes until the peppers are beginning to soften.

Add the diced potato, Serrano ham and butter beans and pour in the chicken stock and saffron-infused stock. Bring to the boil and season to taste. Reduce the heat and simmer for about 10 minutes until the potatoes are cooked. The stew can be prepared to this point ahead of time.

Just before you are about to serve, return the pan to the heat and tip in the cockles or mussels. Cover with a lid. They will open in the heat. Cook for 2–4 minutes. Taste the sauce and season with salt and pepper.

Serve in deep soup bowls, topped with finely chopped fresh tomato and parsley. Accompany with crusty sourdough bread to mop up the juices.

* Alternatively, soak 220g dried butter or cannellini beans in cold water overnight. Next day, pour off the soaking liquid and return the beans to the pan with a bouquet garni, a chunk of onion and a few chunks of carrot. Cover with fresh water, bring to the boil and simmer for 30–45 minutes until just tender. Drain, remove the bouquet garni and flavourings and continue as above.

Who doesn't love these South Indian flavours? Mahi-mahi, a type of tuna, is the preferred fish for this dish in Kerala, but monkfish works brilliantly too. In India it is usual to have lots of 'gravy', or what we call sauce, to flavour the rice deliciously – and a relatively small serving of fish by our standards. If you can't find fresh curry leaves, use dried ones instead – but do keep an eye out for fresh leaves. When you find them, buy more than you need and freeze the surplus. Frozen curry leaves taste altogether better than dried. This curry base reheats extremely well, but don't cook the monkfish and rice until the last minute.

Keralan fish curry

- 40g dry tamarind
- 60g coconut oil
- 3 tablespoons chopped shallot
- 1½ tablespoons grated fresh ginger
- 3 green chillies, split lengthways
- 120g basmati rice
- 1 teaspoon black mustard seeds
- 1 tablespoon fresh curry leaves
- 1 teaspoon ground turmeric
- 1½ teaspoons granulated sugar
- ¾–1 teaspoon chilli powder
- 1½ teaspoons ground coriander
- 800ml fresh coconut milk
  or 2 x 400ml tins of coconut milk
- 600g monkfish (prepared weight),
  cut into 5cm pieces
- 50–100ml boiling water or homemade
  fish stock
- juice of ½–1 organic lime
- flaky sea salt, to taste

To prepare the tamarind water, place the tamarind in a small Pyrex bowl, cover with 75ml boiling water and set aside to soak for 30 minutes to 1 hour. (Make sure the water covers the tamarind completely.) Strain through a sieve, discarding the pips and reserving the strained tamarind water.

Heat the coconut oil in a 25cm sauté pan over a low heat and gently fry the shallots, ginger and green chillies for 5 minutes until they start to colour.

Stir in the rice, mustard seeds, curry leaves, turmeric, sugar, chilli powder and coriander and cook for 2 minutes, stirring, taking care not to burn the spices or they will become bitter.

Add the coconut milk and tamarind water and season to taste with salt. Bring to the boil, cover with a lid and simmer for 4 minutes.

Carefully tuck the pieces of monkfish into the pan, cover and cook for 5–6 minutes until the rice and monkfish are both beautifully cooked. Remove the pan from the heat and set aside, still tightly covered with the lid, for 5–10 minutes. If you feel that the rice has soaked up too much of the sauce, add 50–100ml boiling water or fish stock to loosen the texture. Squeeze in the lime juice and season to taste. Serve with a salad of organic leaves, if you wish.

A gorgeous light fish stew, this dish is perfect for a dinner party. I love it with little aioli crostini, but of course you could serve it with some rice, orzo or pasta.

Mediterranean shellfish stew *with aioli crostini*

- 3 tablespoons extra virgin olive oil
- 1 onion, sliced
- 3 garlic cloves, sliced
- 1 small red chilli, deseeded and chopped
- 150ml dry white wine
- 700g ripe, peeled tomatoes, chopped
  or 1 x 400g tin of tomatoes and
  4 fresh tomatoes, chopped
- 12 mussels, cleaned and debearded
- 12 clams or cockles, cleaned and
  debearded
- 12 raw Dublin Bay prawns, peeled
- 12 scallops, cut in half, or 12 collops
  of monkfish, 2cm thick (or a mixture)
- 1 tablespoon chopped chives
- 2 tablespoons chopped flat-leaf parsley
- 1 tablespoon chopped chervil
- flaky sea salt and freshly ground
  black pepper
- 4–6 slices of baguette, 5mm thick,
  to serve

FOR THE AIOLI
- 2 organic, free-range egg yolks
- 1–2 garlic cloves
- a pinch of English mustard or
  ¼ teaspoon Dijon mustard
- ¼ teaspoon flaky sea salt
- 2 teaspoons white wine vinegar
- 250ml oil, such as sunflower, groundnut
  or olive oil or a mixture (I use
  175ml groundnut oil and 75ml olive oil)
- 2 teaspoons chopped flat-leaf parsley

Heat the olive oil in a 25cm/3.2-litre casserole over a medium heat and cook the onion, garlic and chilli until soft but not coloured. Add the wine and boil for 3–4 minutes then add the tomatoes, reduce the heat to low and cook for 25 minutes.

Meanwhile, make the aioli. Put the egg yolks into a bowl with the garlic, mustard, salt and vinegar. Pour the oil(s) into a measuring jug. Taking a whisk in one hand and the oil in the other, carefully drip the oil onto the egg yolks, drop by drop, whisking at the same time. Within a minute, you will notice that the mixture is beginning to thicken. When this happens, you can add the oil a little faster – but don't get too cheeky or it will suddenly curdle because the egg yolks can only absorb the oil at a certain pace.* Once all of the oil has been incorporated, beat in the parsley. Taste and add a little more seasoning and vinegar, if necessary.

Add the mussels and clams or cockles to the pan and cook for 1–2 minutes before adding the prawns and scallops or monkfish. Cover with a lid and cook for about 4 minutes or until the mussels and clams are wide open and the prawns and scallops or monkfish are opaque. Discard any shells that haven't opened.

Toast the bread for the crostini and top with a dollop of aioli. Keep the remainder covered in the fridge for 7–10 days.

Season the stew to taste and sprinkle with the herbs. Serve with the aioli crostini.

*Good to know

If the aioli curdles, it will suddenly become quite thin. If this happens you can quite easily remedy the situation by cracking another egg yolk into a clean bowl and whisking in the curdled aioli, half a teaspoon at a time.

A sublime way to cook beautiful fresh scallops, the ginger and chervil butter enhances the sweetness of the shellfish. You could cook the scallops in a gratin dish, but it's nicer to leave them in the scallop shells. I also like to add a teaspoon of smoked paprika instead or just use fresh thyme leaves.

Roast scallops *with* ginger & chervil butter

- 8 large scallops on the rounded half shell, if available
- 5cm piece of fresh ginger, finely grated
- 1 teaspoon finely chopped chervil and thyme leaves
- 30g softened butter
- 3 tablespoons extra virgin olive oil
- flaky sea salt and freshly ground black pepper
- organic lemon wedges, to serve

Preheat the oven to 250°C/gas mark 9.

If the scallops are live, open the shell and remove the fringe and everything except the coral and muscle. Wash well. Put the scallops back into the rounded half shells and arrange on a baking tray.

Combine the ginger, chopped chervil or thyme, softened butter and extra virgin olive oil in a small bowl. Spoon a teaspoon of the herby butter onto each scallop and season with a little salt and pepper.

Bake in the very hot oven for 4–5 minutes until the butter is sizzling and the scallops are barely cooked. (A very hot grill works also.) Serve immediately, accompanied by the lemon wedges and some crusty bread to mop up every drop of the delicious juices.

Variation

SCALLOPS WITH SMOKED PAPRIKA & ESPELETTE PEPPER

Substitute smoked paprika for ginger, chervil or thyme in the butter. Slice each scallop into three rounds, arrange 6 rounds, slightly overlapping, in each shell. Put a couple of teaspoons of paprika butter on top, pop under a grill, cook for 4–5 minutes or until the butter is sizzling, sprinkle with a few flakes of espelette pepper and garnish with a sprig of chervil. Alternatively cook in a 21 x 29cm gratin dish.

Grey mullet, sea bass, monkfish, trout or salmon are all quite delicious served in this way. Each person should have the special delight of opening their own parcel with its tantalising aroma. A little hollandaise sauce, which can be made while the fish is cooking, turns this into a feast.

Fish in paper parcels
with cucumber & dill

- 4 x 110g pieces of trout, wild salmon, grey sea mullet, sea bass or monkfish, skinned
- 2 tablespoons chopped dill
- 50g butter
- ½ cucumber, thinly sliced
- flaky sea salt and freshly ground black pepper

Variation

SALMON WITH COURGETTES & GINGER & CHERVIL BUTTER

Take 4 x 110g pieces of wild salmon and sprinkle all over with salt; set aside for 10 minutes. To make the ginger and chervil butter, cream 50g softened butter with 2 teaspoons of chopped chervil, ½ teaspoon of grated fresh ginger, a good squeeze of organic lemon juice and a little black pepper. Grease the parchment paper with butter, as before. Slice 120g courgettes very thinly and arrange half over the buttered side of the parchment paper. Lay the pieces of fish on top and cover with more overlapping slices of courgette. Top with a spoonful of the chervil butter and proceed as above.

Preheat the oven to 180°C/gas mark 4.

Salt the fish on both sides and set aside for 10 minutes, if possible. Dip both sides of the fish in the chopped dill.

Fold four pieces of parchment paper measuring approx. 30 x 25cm in half and smear one half of each piece with a little butter.

Arrange the pieces of fish on the buttered side of the paper. Top each piece of fish with overlapping slices of cucumber and season with freshly ground pepper. Place a small knob of butter on top of the cucumber slices.

Fold the paper over the fish and wrap tightly to seal the edges. Put these parcels on a roasting tray. Cook for 6–10 minutes until the fish is just cooked through. Serve immediately.

A master recipe which we use for almost any round fish, such as cod, pollock, ling, haddock or grey mullet. This perfect one-pot dish can be cooked ahead and reheated – just make sure there's lots of cheese sauce, otherwise it'll be dry and uninteresting instead of juicy and unctuous. Mussels, shrimps, periwinkles or prawns can be added to make for a more elaborate and expensive version. Buttered leeks, peperonata, sautéed mushrooms or tomato fondue are other options – simply put a tablespoon or two either on top of the fish or underneath it in the dish.

Cod, hake or haddock
with dill & pangrattato

- 1.1kg cod, hake, haddock or grey mullet fillets
- 2 bay leaves
- 15g butter
- 600ml whole milk
- approx. 50g roux (made by blending 25g softened butter with 25g plain flour in a small bowl)
- ¼ teaspoon Dijon mustard
- 150–175g grated Cheddar cheese or 75g grated Parmesan cheese
- 1 tablespoon chopped dill (optional)
- flaky sea salt and freshly ground black pepper

FOR THE PANGRATTATO
- 50–75ml extra virgin olive oil
- 1 garlic clove, finely chopped
- 50g soft white breadcrumbs

Preheat the oven to 180°C/gas mark 4.

To make the pangrattato, combine all the ingredients in a little bowl and set aside.

Skin the fish and cut it into 6 or 8 portions. Season with salt and pepper.

Place the bay leaves in a lightly buttered sauté pan or gratin dish and lay the pieces of fish on top. Cover with the milk and bring slowly to the boil. Simmer for 4–5 minutes or until the fish changes from translucent to opaque. Remove the fish with a slotted spoon to a plate and set aside.

Bring the milk back to the boil and whisk in the roux to thicken the sauce to a light coating consistency. Stir in the mustard and two-thirds of the grated cheese, and season to taste with salt and pepper. Add the dill, if using.

Return the fish to the pan and sprinkle the remaining cheese over the top, followed by the pangrattato.

Cook in the oven for 15–20 minutes or until the fish is heated through and the top is golden brown and crisp. Serve with a salad of organic leaves.

Bourride is far less well-known than the legendary French fish soup, bouillabaisse. Some versions purée the base of the soup, others add some tomato dice and mussels and occasionally potato. I love this version, but every Provençale grandmère and chef has their own.

Bourride *with saffron mayo*

- 50ml extra virgin olive oil
- 175g onion, chopped
- 4 leeks, use white and pale green parts (save dark green leaves for stock), diced or cut into 3–5mm slices
- 350g fennel, cut into approx. 2cm dice
- 175g carrots, peeled and cut into approx. 2cm dice
- 500g potatoes, sliced or cut into approx. 2.5cm dice
- 1 bay leaf
- 150ml dry white wine
- 900ml homemade fish stock
- a good pinch of saffron threads, soaked in 2 tablespoons stock
- thinly sliced zest of 1 organic orange
- 1.8kg haddock or monkfish tail on the bone (or a mixture), cut into steaks 4cm thick, across the bone
- 250g peeled shrimps or prawns (optional)
- flaky sea salt, freshly ground black pepper and a good pinch of cayenne pepper
- chervil or flat-leaf parsley sprigs, to serve

FOR THE SAFFRON MAYO
- 2 organic, free-range egg yolks
- 1–4 garlic cloves, crushed with ¼ teaspoon salt
- ¼ teaspoon Dijon mustard
- 2 teaspoons white wine vinegar
- 225ml sunflower, groundnut or olive oil or a mixture
- ½ teaspoon saffron threads, soaked in 1 dessertspoon water
- 2 teaspoons chopped flat-leaf parsley (optional)

Heat the olive oil in a saucepan, add the onion, leek, fennel, carrots, potatoes and bay leaf. Season well with salt and pepper. Cover and cook over a gentle heat for 8–10 minutes, add the dry white wine, increase the heat and continue to cook for 4–5 minutes or until the wine is reduced. Add the hot fish stock and saffron. Return to the boil, add the orange zest, fish and shrimps or prawns, if raw. (Add later if cooked.)

Return to the boil and simmer very gently for 3–5 minutes until the fish is just cooked. Remove the orange peel and bay leaf. (The dish can be prepared ahead to this point.)

To make the saffron mayo, put the egg yolks into a bowl with the garlic salt, mustard and the vinegar (keep the whites to make meringues). Put the oil into a measuring jug. Take a whisk in one hand and the oil in the other and drip the oil onto the egg yolks, drop by drop, whisking at the same time. Within a minute you will notice that the mixture is beginning to thicken. When this happens, you can add the oil a little faster, but don't get too cheeky or it will suddenly curdle because the egg yolks can only absorb the oil at a certain pace. Add the saffron and parsley. Stir to combine. Taste and add a little more seasoning and vinegar if necessary.

Whisk 50ml of the broth into half the saffron mayo. Stir gently into the bourride. Season to taste and serve in wide soup bowls with chervil or parsley. Serve the remaining mayo, toasted baguette or sourdough as accompaniments.

SERVES 2

A very simple 'master recipe', which can be used
not only for plaice, turbot or brill but also for other
flat fish, such as dabs. flounder, sole and lemon sole.
Depending on the size of the fish, you can serve this
recipe as a starter or a main course. It's also delicious
served with hollandaise sauce, mousseline or beurre
blanc in place of the herb butter.

Baked plaice, turbot or brill
with potatoes, fennel & herb butter

- 450g potatoes, peeled and thinly sliced
- 175g onions, thinly sliced
- ½ fennel bulb, very thinly sliced
- extra virgin olive oil, for drizzling
- 1 x 1–1.75kg fresh plaice, turbot, brill
  or other flat fish on the bone
- flaky sea salt and freshly ground
  black pepper

FOR THE HERB BUTTER
- 110g softened butter
- 4 teaspoons finely chopped mixed
  herbs, such as flat-leaf parsley,
  chives, fennel and thyme leaves

Preheat the oven to 250°C/gas mark 9.

Toss together the thinly sliced potatoes, onions and fennel in
a bowl. Drizzle lightly with extra virgin olive oil, season with
salt and spread evenly on an approx. 30 x 50cm baking tray.
Bake for 5 minutes while you prepare the fish.

Turn the fish on its side and remove the head if you wish; I
prefer to leave the fish whole. Wash the fish and clean the slit
by the head very thoroughly. Using a sharp knife, cut through
the skin right around the fish, just where the 'fringe' meets the
flesh. Be careful to cut neatly and to cross the side cuts at the
tail or it will be difficult to remove the skin later on.

Season both sides of the fish with salt and pepper and lay on
top of the partly cooked vegetables. Bake for 17–20 minutes
until the vegetables are tender and the fish is cooked. To
check if the fish is cooked, lift the flesh from the bone at the
head: once it is ready, it should lift off the bone easily and be
quite white with no traces of pink.

To make the herb butter, mix the softened butter in a little
bowl with the herbs.

Just before you are about to serve, catch the skin down near
the tail of the fish and pull it off gently (the skin will tear
badly if it hasn't been properly cut). Lift the two fillets onto
a hot plate and coat with the herb butter. Raise the tail and
carefully lift the bone off the remainder of the fish. Break at
the head and put aside. Carefully lift the remaining two fillets
onto the plate. Coat with the herb butter and surround with
the potatoes, onions and fennel, which should be deliciously
charred at the edges. Serve immediately.

Fishcakes are absolutely delicious when they are carefully made and served hot with a small blob of herb or garlic butter melting on top. Try them here with spring onion aioli. Don't be afraid to experiment – a little horseradish cream added to the fishcakes gives extra oomph! I have also experimented with a little grated ginger and chopped dill or lemongrass. For a spicy variation, follow the recipe below and add 1–2 deseeded and chopped chillies with the onion. You could also substitute freshly chopped coriander for the parsley if you wish. Accompany with a tomato and chilli sauce and garnish with sprigs of fresh coriander.

Fishcakes *with spring onion aioli*

- 25g butter
- 110g onions, finely chopped
- 110g mashed potato
- 750g cold leftover fish, such as salmon, cod, haddock or hake (a proportion of smoked fish, such as smoked haddock or mackerel, is good)
- 1 organic, free-range egg yolk or small egg
- 1 tablespoon chopped flat-leaf parsley
- seasoned plain flour, for dusting
- 1 beaten organic, free-range egg, for coating
- 50–75g fresh white breadcrumbs or panko crumbs
- 25g butter (preferably clarified, see page 16)
- 2 tablespoons extra virgin olive oil
- flaky sea salt and freshly ground black pepper

FOR THE SPRING ONION AIOLI
- ½ x quantity Aioli (page 96)
- 2 tablespoons finely chopped spring onions (both white and green parts)

To make the fishcakes, melt the butter in a frying pan, stir in the onion and sweat over a gentle heat, covered, for 4–5 minutes until soft but not coloured. Scrape the contents of the pan into a bowl and carefully stir in the mashed potato, flaked cooked fish, egg and chopped parsley. Season to taste with salt and pepper. Form the mixture into fishcakes, approx. 50g each or larger if you prefer. Coat each one first in the seasoned flour, then in the beaten egg and finally in the breadcrumbs. Set aside on a plate and chill until needed.

To make the aioli, combine the aioli with the chopped spring onions in a bowl.

Heat the butter and oil in the frying pan over a low to medium heat and fry the fishcakes for about 3 minutes (depending on thickness), on each side until heated through and golden. Serve piping hot with a blob of spring onion aioli on top. A good green salad and some Tomato Fondue (page 133) make perfect accompaniments.

One of my favourite monkfish dishes. Hake, haddock
or wild salmon also work here, but cut the fish into
individual portions rather than chunks. Serve with lots
of rice or pasta to mop up the delicious juices.

Monkfish poached
with tomatoes & Swiss chard

- 1kg monkfish, well-trimmed and cut
  into 125g pieces
- 350g Swiss chard
- 4 tablespoons extra virgin olive oil
- 110g onions, peeled and cut in half
  lengthways, then cut crossways into
  fine half rings
- 50g piece of fresh ginger, peeled and
  cut into very fine slivers
- 1 x 400g tin of plum tomatoes,
  chopped, with their juice
- 110ml thick coconut milk
- 150ml water
- flaky sea salt, freshly ground black
  pepper and a sprinkling of pul biber

Season both sides of the monkfish pieces with salt, pepper
and a sprinkling of pul biber. Set aside for 15 minutes.

Remove the central stems from the Swiss chard and cut them
crossways into strips 3mm wide. Roll the green leaves and cut
crossways into strips 5mm wide.

Heat the oil in a wide sauté pan over a medium-high heat.
When it is hot, add the onions, ginger and chard stems and
sauté for 5 minutes, stirring. Add the chopped tomatoes and
continue to cook for a further 5 minutes. Pour in the coconut
milk and water, and season with 1 teaspoon of salt and some
pepper. Bring to the boil, stirring, then simmer over a low heat
for 1 minute. The recipe can be prepared to this point ahead of
time and reheated.

To serve, bring the sauce to a simmer once again. Stir in the
chard leaves and simmer for a minute or two. Lay the fish in a
single layer over the top of the sauce and spoon some of the
sauce over the fish. Cover with a lid and simmer very gently for
8–10 minutes or until the fish is just cooked through. Season
to taste. Serve with pilaff rice or fresh pasta, if you wish, or just
some good bread to mop up the juices.

An inspired way to cook whole fillets of fish, I've given three separate sauce suggestions here but even a simple dill butter makes roast fish into a feast. Needless to say, other fish, such as haddock, hake, ling, cod or pollock can be cooked in exactly the same way.

Roast fish *three ways*

- 1 whole wild fresh salmon
- melted butter or extra virgin olive oil, about 25g/25ml
- flaky sea salt and freshly ground black pepper

FOR THE TOMATO & DILL TOPPING
- 4–8 tablespoons chopped dill
- 4–6 ripe tomatoes, deseeded and diced, sprinkled with a little flaky sea salt, freshly ground black pepper and sugar
- 110–225g extra virgin olive oil

Preheat the oven to 250°C/gas mark 9.

Descale the salmon, fillet and remove the pin bones. For the topping, mix the dill and diced seasoned tomato together with the extra virgin olive oil.

Line a baking tray with parchment paper. Put the fillets of fish on top. Brush with the melted butter or extra virgin olive oil and season with salt and pepper. Spoon the dill and tomato oil over the surface. Roast for 8–10 minutes or until cooked and tender.

Serve in the tray or transfer the salmon onto one or two hot serving dishes. Sprinkle with a little fresh dill and dill flowers. Serve immediately with a salad of organic green leaves.

Variations

ROAST SALMON WITH TERIYAKI SAUCE
To make the teriyaki sauce, put 100ml light or dark soy sauce, 100ml dry white wine, 2 large, thinly sliced garlic cloves, a 4cm piece of fresh ginger, peeled and thinly sliced, 2 tablespoons of wholegrain mustard and 2 tablespoons of soft brown sugar into a stainless-steel saucepan. Bring to the boil and simmer for 3–4 minutes. (Alternatively, spoon over the fish before putting it in the oven.) Roast the fish as above. Brush the fish generously with the teriyaki sauce, sprinkle with fresh coriander and serve.

ROAST SALMON WITH PUL BIBER
Prepare the salmon as above, drizzle with extra virgin olive oil. Sprinkle with pul biber and flaky sea salt. Roast as above. Serve with a good green salad.

This is a tradition in San Francisco, but I first enjoyed it at my friend Mary Risley's table, who ran Tante Marie's Cooking School. She kindly shared the recipe for this substantial meal in a pot – you'll love it. All you need is some bread for dunking.

Californian cioppino

- 24 well-scrubbed live clams or cockles
- 2 onions, chopped
- 2 tablespoons extra virgin olive oil, plus extra to drizzle
- 3 garlic cloves, chopped
- 1 fennel bulb, chopped
- 1.1kg fresh tomatoes, peeled (see page 112), deseeded and chopped or 3 x 400g tins of Italian plum tomatoes
- 1 tablespoon tomato purée (optional)
- 450ml dry white wine
- ½ teaspoon red pepper flakes
- 1¾ tablespoons chopped oregano or annual marjoram
- 900g fresh white fish, such as sea bass, rock cod, halibut or monkfish
- 450g scallops (optional)
- 450g raw shrimps or prawns
- brown and white meat from 1 large cooked crab (optional)
- 25g flat-leaf parsley, chopped
- flaky sea salt and freshly ground black pepper
- sourdough bread, to serve

First steam the clams or cockles. Place them in a heavy-bottomed pot with 2.5cm of water. Cover and cook over a high heat, shaking occasionally, until the shells open. Set aside in a bowl, reserving the broth, and keep covered until ready to use.

To make the soup base, put the onions into the pot with ½ teaspoon of salt and a generous splash of olive oil. Cook, stirring from time to time, until the onions are soft. Stir in the garlic and cook for another minute or two. Add the fennel, tomatoes, tomato purée, wine, red pepper flakes and oregano.

Carefully strain the broth from the steamed clams into the pot, leaving behind the last tablespoon or so as it will probably be very gritty. Bring to the boil, stirring, and simmer gently for 20 minutes.

Meanwhile, cut the white fish into large chunks, drizzle lightly with olive oil and season with salt and pepper.

Remove the muscle from each scallop and peel the shrimps. Place the shellfish on a clean plate, drizzle lightly with olive oil and season with salt and pepper.

About 15 minutes before you are ready to serve, bring the soup base to the boil, stirring. Carefully fold in the chunks of white fish, cover with a lid and simmer for 5 minutes.

Carefully fold in the scallops and shrimps and simmer gently for a further 5 minutes. Stir in the steamed clams and crab meat, if using.

Season to taste. Then cover the pan with a lid and set aside for a minute or two.

Sprinkle with lots of parsley and serve in warmed bowls with sourdough bread to mop up all the juices.

Who doesn't love a fish pie? This easy-peasy recipe can be used for almost any round fish, including cod, pollock, ling, haddock, salmon or grey mullet. I like to prepare a big batch to make several pies, which can be refrigerated or frozen and reheated another day. A chopped hard-boiled egg and 110g cooked peas add extra nourishment and flavour. Here I use a scrunchy filo topping, but I often make a crispy Cheddar crumb or mashed potato topping.

Mermaid's fish pie

- 1.1kg cod, hake, haddock or grey mullet fillets, or a mixture
- 15g butter, for greasing
- 600ml whole milk
- approx. 20g roux (made by blending 10g softened butter with 10g plain flour)
- ¼ teaspoon Dijon mustard
- 150–175g grated Gruyère or Cheddar cheese or 75g grated Parmesan cheese
- 2 tablespoons chopped flat-leaf parsley
- 110g shelled cooked mussels
- 110g peeled cooked shrimps
- ½ tin of chopped anchovies, approx. 4 fillets (optional)
- 4 sheets of filo pastry
- melted butter, for brushing
- flaky sea salt and freshly ground black pepper

Variations
MERMAID'S FISH PIE WITH SEAWEED BUTTER
Cream 110g softened butter with 2 tablespoons of finely chopped dulse and a few drops of lemon juice in a small bowl. Shape into a butter pat and form into a roll. Wrap in greaseproof paper or tin foil, screwing each end so that it looks like a Christmas cracker. Refrigerate to harden. Cut into 6–8 portions and serve with the fish pie.

Preheat the oven to 180°C/gas mark 4.

Skin the fish and cut into 6-8 portions. Season well with salt and pepper. Lay the pieces of fish in a lightly buttered 26cm sauté pan and cover with cold milk. Bring to the boil, then simmer for 4–5 minutes until the fish has changed from translucent to opaque. Remove the fish to a plate with a slotted spoon.

Bring the milk back to the boil and whisk in enough of the roux to thicken the sauce to a light coating consistency. Stir in the mustard, grated cheese and chopped parsley. Season to taste with salt and pepper. Add the cooked fish together with the mussels, shrimps and chopped anchovies, and stir gently to coat with the sauce.

Brush each filo sheet with melted butter and cut into four pieces. Scrunch up each piece of filo pastry and arrange side by side on top of the pie.

Bake in the oven for 15-20 minutes until the pie is bubbling and the filo is crisp and crunchy.

Hake, cod, or monkfish also work deliciously with this sweet pepper stew. Add 225g diced cooked potato to the base for an extra-filling supper.

Spanish red pepper stew *with haddock*

- 2 tablespoons extra virgin olive oil, plus extra to serve
- 1 garlic clove, crushed
- 225g onions, sliced
- 40ml dry sherry
- 4 red peppers
- 1 red or green chilli, sliced
- 6 large tomatoes (dark red and very ripe)
- a pinch of saffron threads
- a few fresh basil leaves
- 4 x 175g haddock fillets
- 1–2 teaspoons smoked paprika
- flaky sea salt, freshly ground black pepper and sugar
- plenty of chopped flat-leaf parsley, to serve

Heat 2 tablespoons of olive oil over a gentle heat in a 25cm/3.2-litre casserole, add the garlic and cook for a few seconds. Add the sliced onions, toss in the oil and soften over a gentle heat for 5–6 minutes. Pour in the sherry, bring to the boil and reduce for 5–6 minutes.

Halve the peppers, removing the seeds and stalks. Cut the peppers into quarters and then into 2–2.5cm squares. Add to the pan with the chilli and stir to combine. Cover with a lid and cook for 5–6 minutes while you prepare the tomatoes.

Scald the tomatoes in boiling water for 10 seconds, then pour off the water and slip off the skins. Slice the tomatoes and add to the stew with the saffron. Season with salt, pepper and sugar, and throw in the basil. Cook for 20 minutes, covered, until the vegetables are just soft. It should be sweet and juicy.

Season the fish fillets with salt, pepper and some smoked paprika. Lay the fish on top of the softened vegetables, cover with a lid and cook for 4–5 minutes until the fish changes from translucent to opaque. Sprinkle a little more smoked paprika over the top of each piece of fish.

Serve as soon as possible, scattered with parsley and drizzled with extra virgin olive oil. Accompany with lots of crusty sourdough and a good salad of organic leaves.

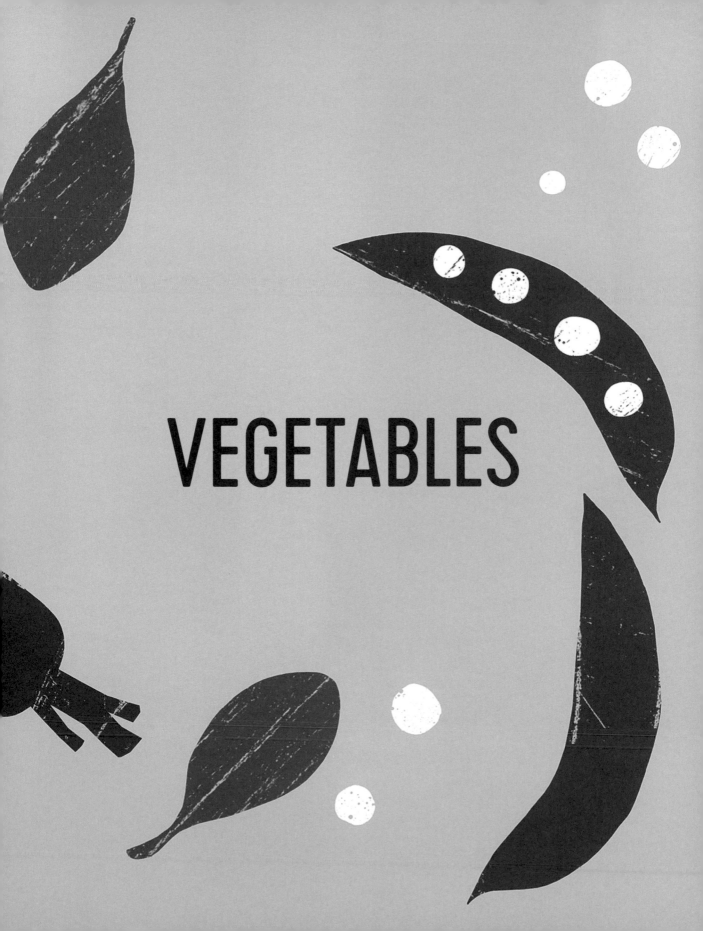

VEGETABLES

SERVES 8

This recipe is based on a thick unctuous soup that Naomi Duguid and her friends cooked for lunch at the Oxford Food Symposium 2018. I'm crazy about purslane and try to encourage everyone I meet to grow it. Once established, it spreads rapidly so be careful where you plant it. I use it in a million different ways – in soups, salads, stews... It's very nutritious and grows wild in many areas. I've heard that it's classed as a noxious weed in the USA – it even grows up through cracks in the pavement – but my answer would just be to eat it. Few foods are so full of good things as this juicy little succulent.

Purslane soup

- 225g Puy lentils, rinsed and picked over
- 55g onions, finely chopped
- 100g arborio or other short-grain rice, washed and drained
- 1.8 litres vegetable stock or water
- 3 tablespoons tomato purée
- 1 teaspoon ground cumin
- ½ teaspoon ground turmeric
- 3 teaspoons sea salt, to taste (you may need more)
- 275g purslane leaves and stems, finely chopped
- coarsely cracked black pepper
- extra virgin olive oil, to drizzle

TO SERVE
- 8 warm flatbreads
- 125g hard goat's or sheep's cheese, crumbled
- 8 organic lemon wedges
- a generous quantity of fresh herbs: I use little sprigs of flat-leaf parsley, tarragon, chervil, mint and lovage together with a few spring onions, sliced on the diagonal

Put the lentils, onions and rice into a 25cm/3.2-litre saucepan and cover with 1.8 litres stock (or water, as a last resort). Bring to a rolling boil, stirring all the time. Skim off any foam that forms on the surface, then cover and reduce the heat to a gentle simmer. Cook for 20 minutes, covered, until the lentils are tender – you might need to add a little more stock or water, if necessary.

Stir in the tomato purée, cumin, turmeric and 2 teaspoons of salt, then add the purslane and stir thoroughly. Cook for about 20 minutes or until the purslane is very soft and the flavours have blended. Season to taste. The soup should be thick and unctuous, but if you prefer a thinner soup you could add a further 300ml stock.

Ladle into individual bowls, sprinkle with coarsely cracked black pepper and drizzle with extra virgin olive oil. Bring the flatbreads, cheese, lemon wedges and sprigs of fresh herbs to the table and let everyone add their own toppings.

This is a gorgeous aubergine dish. The spiced aubergine mixture is also good served cold or at room temperature as an accompaniment to hot or cold lamb or pork. We grow several varieties of aubergine at Ballymaloe, but look out for Slim Jim for this dish – it's one of my favourites. You can add 450g diced cooked potatoes instead of the chickpeas, if you wish, but you'll also need to add 150ml vegetable or chicken stock to keep the sauce nice and juicy.

Spiced aubergine *with goat's cheese, chickpeas & rocket*

- 2.5cm piece of fresh ginger, peeled and coarsely chopped
- 6 large garlic cloves, coarsely crushed
- 50ml water
- approx. 250ml extra virgin olive oil
- 800g aubergines, cut into slices 2cm thick
- 1 teaspoon whole fennel seeds
- 2 teaspoons whole cumin seeds
- 350g very ripe tomatoes, peeled and finely chopped or 1 x 400g tin of chopped tomatoes, plus 1 teaspoon sugar
- 1 tablespoon ground coriander
- ¼ teaspoon ground turmeric
- ½ teaspoon cayenne pepper
- 55g raisins
- 1 x 400g tin of chickpeas, drained and rinsed
- 110g soft goat's cheese
- fresh rocket leaves
- flaky sea salt
- lots of crusty bread, to serve (optional)

Put the ginger, garlic and water into a blender and blend until fairly smooth.

Heat 175ml oil in a 25–30cm sauté pan. When it is hot and almost smoking, add a few of the aubergine slices and cook until tender and golden on both sides. Remove and drain on a wire rack over a baking sheet. Repeat with the remaining aubergine, adding more oil if necessary.

Heat 3 tablespoons oil in the pan. When hot, add the fennel and cumin seeds – careful not to let them burn – and stir just for a few seconds. Put in the chopped tomatoes, the ginger-garlic mixture, the ground coriander and turmeric, a pinch of cayenne and some salt. Simmer for 5–6 minutes, stirring occasionally, until the mixture thickens slightly.

Add the fried aubergine slices, raisins and chickpeas, and stir gently to coat them in the spicy sauce. Cover the pan with a lid, reduce the heat to very low and cook for 3–4 minutes. The dish can be prepared ahead to this point.

To serve, drop dollops of the soft goat's cheese over the surface, scatter with some fresh rocket leaves and drizzle with a little extra virgin olive oil. Serve warm with lots of crusty bread, if you wish.

This gorgeous tart was inspired by a photo on the cover of *Delicious* magazine. The ricotta and pecorino filling is uncooked, so be sure to assemble the tart close to the time of eating. Best made in late summer or early autumn when the tomatoes are exquisitely sweet. I use the delicious buffalo ricotta made in West Cork for this dish.

Heirloom tomato & ricotta tart

FOR THE PASTRY
- 150g plain white flour
- 75g cold butter
- a little water, to bind
- 1 beaten organic, free-range egg, to seal

FOR THE FILLING
- 250g buffalo ricotta
- 100g pecorino cheese, grated
- 2 tablespoons double cream
- 1 tablespoon extra virgin olive oil
- 1 tablespoon honey
- 2 tablespoons chopped basil, thyme and marjoram, plus extra leaves to garnish
- zest of ½ organic lemon
- flaky sea salt
- ¼ teaspoon freshly cracked black pepper
- 650g mixed heritage and cherry tomatoes, including striped zebra (green), red and yellow cherry tomatoes, if available

First make the pastry. All the ingredients should be cold. Sift the flour into a large bowl. Cut the butter into cubes. Toss the cubes into the flour and then proceed to lift up a few cubes of butter at the time in each hand. Using your thumbs, rub the cubes of butter across the middle three fingers, towards the index fingers.

Allow the flakes of floured butter to drop back into the bowl, then pick up some more and continue until all the butter is rubbed in. As you rub in the butter, hold your hands well above the bowl and run your fingers through the flour to incorporate as much air as possible to keep the mixture cool. This whole process should only take a minute or two – careful not to rub the butter in too much, or the pastry will be heavy. The pieces should resemble lumpy breadcrumbs. If you are in doubt, shake the bowl and any larger pieces will come to the top. Add salt if using unsalted butter.

Using a fork, toss and stir the pastry as you add just enough water to bind – 2–3 tablespoons should do the trick. If you are in doubt, discard the fork and collect up the pastry with your hand as you will be able to judge more easily by feel if it needs a little more water. Careful not to make the pastry too wet or it will shrink in the oven. If the pastry is too dry, it will be difficult to roll out.

When the pastry has come together, turn it out onto the work surface and flatten it into an approx. 30cm round. Cover with greaseproof paper or clingfilm and, if possible, set aside in the fridge to rest for at least 15 minutes to allow the gluten to relax. The pastry will then be less likely to shrink in the oven.

Preheat the oven to 180°C/gas mark 4.

Roll out the pastry to a circle approx. 25cm in diameter.
Lift the pastry over a 23cm greased tart tin and press down
gently around the sides. Trim around the edges with a sharp
knife and prick the base gently with a fork. Line with baking
parchment and fill with baking beans.

Transfer the pastry case to the oven and bake 'blind' for
about 25 minutes until pale and golden. Remove the baking
beans and paper. Brush the part-baked pastry case all over
with a little beaten egg and pop it back into the oven for 5–10
minutes until pale golden brown all over. Set aside to cool.

To make the filling, combine the ricotta and pecorino in a
bowl. Add the double cream, extra virgin olive oil, honey,
herbs, lemon zest, salt and pepper. Mix gently together. Taste
a little dollop of the filling with a slice of tomato and correct
the seasoning, if necessary. It might need a little more honey.

Slice the larger tomatoes and cut the smaller cherry ones in
half lengthways or crossways, as you prefer.

Not long before serving, spoon the ricotta filling into the
cooked pastry case and arrange the tomatoes on top. I like to
arrange the sliced, bigger ones, including the green zebra over
the base and top with the smaller cherry tomatoes. Season
with salt, pepper, a little drizzle of honey (about ½ teaspoon)
and lots of thyme and marjoram leaves. Garnish with a few
little basil leaves and serve soon.

One of the very best vegetarian one-pot dishes. What's not to like about black-eyed beans, chickpeas and pumpkin with lots of spices? Delicious on its own, but equally good with a roast chicken or a few lamb chops. Eat with flatbreads or pilaff rice, if you prefer.

Black-eyed bean, pumpkin & chickpea stew

- 6 tablespoons extra virgin olive oil
- 1 teaspoon cumin seeds
- 1 x 2.5cm cinnamon stick
- 150g onions, chopped
- 4 garlic cloves, very finely chopped
- 225g fresh mushrooms, sliced approx. 3mm thick
- 450g pumpkin or butternut squash, peeled and cut in 2cm cubes
- 400g fresh tomatoes, peeled and chopped or 1 x 400g tin of chopped tomatoes
- 2 teaspoons ground coriander
- 1 teaspoon ground cumin
- ½ teaspoon ground turmeric
- a pinch of sugar
- ¼ teaspoon cayenne pepper
- 450g cooked black-eyed beans, strained (reserving the cooking liquid)
- 225g cooked chickpeas, strained (reserving the cooking liquid)
- 1 teaspoon salt
- freshly ground black pepper
- 3 tablespoons chopped coriander

FOR THE MINT YOGURT
- 300ml natural yogurt
- 1 tablespoon chopped mint leaves

Heat the oil in a sauté pan over a medium-high heat. When it is hot, put in the cumin seeds and the cinnamon stick. Let them sizzle for 5–6 seconds, then add the onions and garlic. Stir-fry for 3–4 minutes until the onion is just beginning to colour at the edges. Add the mushrooms and cook until the mushrooms wilt, then add the pumpkin or squash, tomatoes, ground coriander, cumin and turmeric, a pinch of sugar and the cayenne. Cook for 1 minute, stirring, then cover with a lid and cook over a gentle heat for 10 minutes.

Turn off the heat and tip in the drained beans and chickpeas. Add the salt and pepper, together with 2 tablespoons of coriander. Pour in 150ml of bean cooking liquid and 150ml of the chickpea liquid (or 300ml vegetable stock if you've used tinned pulses). Return to the boil, and then reduce the heat and simmer for 10–15 minutes, stirring occasionally, until the beans and chickpeas are tender.

To make the mint yogurt, combine the yogurt with the chopped mint in a bowl.

Remove the cinnamon stick from the pan before serving and sprinkle with the remaining coriander. Spoon into serving bowls and top with a dollop of the mint yogurt. Accompany with a good green salad and rice, if you wish.

A delicious, fresh-tasting vegetarian starter or small plate, bursting with clean fresh flavours. Best eaten immediately, otherwise the vegetable mixture becomes very watery.

Cauliflower ceviche on corn tostado *with chilli mayo & avocado*

- 8 x 10cm crisp corn tostados
- 2 ripe avocados, peeled and cut into chunky slices crossways
- fresh herb sprigs, such as coriander, sweet cicely or flat-leaf parsley, to serve

FOR THE CHILLI MAYONNAISE
- 1½ tablespoons puréed chipotle chillies in adobo
- juice of 1 lime (optional)
- 1 tablespoon chopped coriander
- 225ml homemade mayonnaise
- a pinch of salt

FOR THE 'CEVICHE'
- 4 tablespoons finely diced cauliflower (approx. 5mm)
- 4 tablespoons finely diced cucumber (unpeeled)
- 4 tablespoons finely diced tomato (seeds discarded)
- 2 tablespoons finely diced onion
- 1 teaspoon chopped red chilli, or to taste
- 2 tablespoons roughly chopped coriander
- juice of 1 organic lime
- flaky sea salt and freshly ground black pepper

For the chilli mayo, stir the puréed chipotle chillies in adobo, lime juice and fresh coriander into the mayonnaise and add a pinch of salt.

Mix all the ingredients for the ceviche together in a bowl.

To serve, spread some of the chilli mayo on each tostado, top with a couple of spoonfuls of the cauliflower ceviche and finish with a few slices of avocado and some herbs.

Enjoy immediately.

SERVES 4

At Ballymaloe we make gorgeous thick unctuous yogurt from the milk of our small Jersey herd. I love to serve herb-flavoured yogurt with lots of dishes, such as this one as well as plain rice.

Courgette *with yogurt & fresh herbs*

- 4 courgettes, 12–15cm long
- 4 tablespoons extra virgin olive oil
- 125g thick natural yogurt
- 1 fat garlic clove, crushed or finely grated
- 1 teaspoon runny honey
- lots of freshly snipped herbs, such as dill, chervil and tarragon
- flaky sea salt and freshly ground black pepper
- borage or hyssop flowers (optional), to garnish
- sourdough bread, to serve

Heat a heavy-based griddle pan over a high heat. Slice the courgettes lengthways into 5mm strips. Drizzle with extra virgin olive oil and season with salt and pepper.

Cook a few at a time on the hot pan grill until soft and marked by the grill on both sides. Transfer to a platter and arrange side by side.

Mix the yogurt with the garlic and honey in a small bowl, and season with a little salt.

Drizzle the yogurt mixture generously over the courgettes and scatter with plenty of herb sprigs. Pretty blue borage or hyssop flowers look lovely sprinkled over the top, if available, as, of course, do courgette blossoms.

Serve with crusty sourdough bread.

VEGETABLES 127

Roast cauliflower is a brilliant vehicle for myriad flavours. For minimum effort, just scatter the roasted cauliflower with chopped parsley or a generous dusting of freshly grated Parmesan or frozen blue cheese, which is so easy to grate.

Roast cauliflower *with* *anchovies, peppers & herbs*

- 1 medium cauliflower, weighing approx. 1.4kg
- 75–100g butter
- 2 teaspoons thyme leaves or 1 teaspoon finely chopped rosemary
- salt

FOR THE TOPPING
- 1 tablespoon chopped flat-leaf parsley
- 1 garlic clove, crushed
- 50g Piquillo pepper or ripe cherry tomatoes, chopped
- 15g anchovies, chopped
- 4–6 tablespoons extra virgin olive oil
- 1 teaspoon finely grated organic lemon zest
- 20g toasted flaked almonds

Variation
SPICY CAULIFLOWER
Cook the cauliflower as above. Instead of making the thyme butter, heat 6 tablespoons of extra virgin olive oil, 2 teaspoons of ground cumin, 2 teaspoons of ground coriander, 1 teaspoon of ground turmeric and 1 teaspoon of pul biber in the casserole and cook for 1 minute. Add the cauliflower and baste in the spicy oil before cooking in the oven for 5–6 minutes, uncovered. Sprinkle with sea salt and 2 teaspoons of chopped coriander before serving.

Preheat the oven to 230°C/gas mark 8.

First prepare the cauliflower. Remove the outer leaves from the cauliflower and trim the base. Cut a deep cross in the base, then remove the rest of the leaves and cut the stalk into 4cm pieces. Pour 2cm water into a 22cm ovenproof casserole, approx. 10cm deep, season with plenty of salt and bring to the boil. Put the chopped leaves and stalk into the bottom of the pan and place the cauliflower head on top. Cover the pan with a lid and simmer for 4 minutes, then remove the lid and cook for a further 2 minutes. Remove the cauliflower and leaves to a plate and tip out any water in the pan.

Melt the butter in the casserole and allow it to become golden brown – careful it doesn't burn. Quickly add the thyme leaves, then the cooked cauliflower. Baste the cauliflower with the thyme butter and then transfer the pan to the hot oven to cook for 15–20 minutes, uncovered. Regular basting, though not essential, makes it even more delicious. To test for doneness, pierce the base with a skewer.

Meanwhile, mix all of the ingredients for the topping together in a bowl, apart from the flaked almonds. Spoon the topping over the roasted cauliflower and sprinkle with the toasted, flaked almonds. Serve with crusty bread, if you wish.

Spanakopita can also be made in individual 'snails', but this delicious flaky version comes in a sauté pan. This version is good for a feast as it serves 12–15 people. You can halve the recipe if you're serving smaller numbers.

Spanakopita Greek spinach & cheese pie

- 150g butter
- 900g leeks, sliced and washed really well
- 6 tablespoons extra virgin olive oil
- 500g onions, finely chopped
- 8 spring onions (both white and green parts), finely sliced
- 900g fresh spinach, weighed after the stalks have been removed, washed really well
- 6 tablespoons chopped flat-leaf parsley
- 6 tablespoons chopped dill
- 350g feta cheese, crumbled
- 125g Parmesan cheese, grated
- 4 organic, free-range eggs, beaten
- 9 sheets of filo pastry, 30 x 43cm (about one packet)
- 15g melted butter, for brushing
- egg wash, made by beating 1 organic, free-range egg with 2–3 tablespoons whole milk
- flaky sea salt, freshly ground black pepper and nutmeg

Preheat the oven to 180°C/gas mark 4.

Melt the butter in a 26cm ovenproof sauté pan and cook the sliced leeks with 2–3 tablespoons of water for 4–5 minutes until tender (older leeks may take slightly longer). Scoop the leeks out of the pan and set aside on a plate while you cook the spinach.

Heat the olive oil in the sauté pan, add the onions and spring onions, and sweat over a low heat for 3–4 minutes, covered, until soft but not coloured. Increase the heat to medium, add the spinach and toss well to coat it in the oil. Season with salt, pepper and nutmeg. Add the chopped parsley and dill, and continue to cook for 4–5 minutes, stirring, until the spinach has wilted. Turn out the spinach mixture into a colander and set aside to drain and cool.

Combine the crumbled feta and 100g of the grated Parmesan in a medium bowl and beat in the egg. Add the well-drained spinach and the leeks and season to taste.

Brushing each sheet of filo with melted butter as you go, layer up the pastry in the base of the sauté pan or roasting dish so that it comes up the sides, leaving enough pastry hanging over the sides to fold over and encase the filling.

Spread the filling evenly over the pastry and bring up the sides of the filo to enclose the filling. Score the top of the pie into a diamond or square pattern and brush all over with the egg wash. Sprinkle the surface with the remaining 25g grated Parmesan.

Bake for about 45 minutes until puffed up and golden.

Serve, cut into wedges, while still warm and fluffy.

Cheddar cheese fondue sounds so retro, but it's a brilliant one-pot supper. Choose your seat carefully, because if you drop the bread into the fondue you must kiss the person on your right – this could be your big chance! My mother-in-law, Myrtle Allen, devised this Cheese Fondue recipe made from Irish Cheddar cheese. It's a huge favourite at Ballymaloe, as even though it's a meal in itself it can be made in minutes and is loved by adults and children alike. A fondue set is obviously an advantage, but not totally essential. Florets of cauliflower, Romanesco or broccoli make crunchy dippers.

Ballymaloe Cheddar cheese fondue

- 4 tablespoons dry white wine
- 4 small garlic cloves, crushed
- 4 teaspoons good tomato chutney
  (I use Ballymaloe Relish)
- 4 teaspoons chopped flat-leaf parsley
- 170g mature Cheddar cheese, grated
- lots of crusty white bread, at least
  4 thick slices
- florets of cauliflower, Romanesco or
  broccoli, or a mixture

Put the white wine, garlic, chutney, parsley and cheese into a fondue pot or a small saucepan and stir to combine, off the heat.

Just before you are about to serve the fondue, put the fondue pot or small, heavy-based saucepan over a low heat and cook until the cheese melts and begins to bubble – but don't stir. Transfer the pot to the fondue stove, if available, or use a heatproof stand, a trivet or a mat and serve immediately.

Provide each guest with some fresh slices of bread, or cubes of bread crisped up slightly in a hot oven and a selection of chopped vegetables. They will also need a fondue fork and an ordinary fork.

This is one of my 'go-to' recipes to feed a group of hungry friends. You can replace the chicken with leftover cooked pheasant, fish or shellfish, if you wish – monkfish works particularly well. Just think of the tomato fondue as a base for many good things.

Spicy tomato fondue
with many good things

FOR THE SPICY TOMATO FONDUE

- 2 tablespoons extra virgin olive oil
- 110g onions, sliced
- 1–2 chillies, deseeded and finely chopped
- 2 teaspoons ground cumin
- 1 garlic clove, crushed
- 900g very ripe tomatoes in summer, peeled (see page 112), or 2 x 400g tins of chopped tomatoes in winter
- flaky sea salt, freshly ground black pepper and sugar, to taste

FOR THE 'MANY GOOD THINGS'

- 700–900g cooked chicken, cut into approx. 2.5cm dice
- 6 cooked potatoes, cut into approx. 2cm dice
- lots of coarsely chopped flat-leaf parsley or coriander

First make the tomato fondue. Heat the oil in a large stainless-steel sauté pan or casserole over a gentle heat. Add the sliced onions, chopped chillies, ground cumin and garlic, and stir well to coat everything in the oil. Cover the pan with a lid and sweat over a gentle heat for about 10 minutes until the onions are soft, but not coloured. It is vital that the onions are completely soft before you add the tomatoes.

Slice the peeled fresh tomatoes and add to the pan with their juices (if you are using tinned tomatoes, you can tip them straight in). Season with salt, pepper and sugar; tinned tomatoes need lots of sugar because of their high acidity. Cover and cook for a further 10–20 minutes until the tomato softens, uncovering for the last 5 minutes or so to reduce the sauce a little. Fresh tomatoes need a shorter cooking time than tinned ones to preserve their lively fresh flavour. Depending on how you plan to use your fondue, you might want to reduce it a bit further.

Add the cooked chicken and potatoes, bring to the boil and bubble away for 4–5 minutes. Season to taste and scatter with parsley or coriander.

Serve with a salad of organic green leaves.

SERVES 6

Everyone loves this North Indian vegetarian dish. If you're not too rushed, sauté the cubed paneer in a little oil beforehand until they are lightly coloured, then pop them into a bowl of hot water until you are ready to add them to the sauce. Soaking the fried paneer in water really plumps it up, but make sure you drain it really well before adding it to the sauce. Feta makes a good substitute if you can't get hold of paneer.

Matar paneer curry

- 5g finely grated fresh ginger
- 5g crushed garlic
- 3 tablespoons vegetable oil
- 1 teaspoon cumin seeds
- 100g onions, finely chopped
- 4 ripe tomatoes, finely chopped into 3mm dice
- 1 teaspoon chilli powder
- 1 tablespoon ground coriander
- ½ level teaspoon ground turmeric
- ½ level teaspoon ground fenugreek
- ¾ teaspoon garam masala
- 150g thick natural yogurt or labneh
- 250g paneer or feta cheese, cut into 2.5cm cubes
- 200g fresh or frozen peas
- freshly squeezed organic lime juice, to taste
- salt, to taste
- chopped coriander leaves, to serve

FOR THE CUCUMBER & YOGURT RAITA
- ¼ medium cucumber
- ½ tablespoon finely chopped onion
- ½ teaspoon cumin seeds
- 150ml natural yogurt
- 1 ripe tomato, finely diced (seeds discarded)
- 1 tablespoon chopped coriander leaves
- flaky sea salt and freshly ground black pepper

First make the cucumber and yogurt raita. Peel the cucumber if you wish, cut it in half lengthways and remove the seeds, then cut into 5mm dice. Put the diced cucumber into a bowl with the onion, sprinkle with salt and set aside for 5–10 minutes.

Meanwhile, roast the cumin seeds in a pan to release their aroma, then crush lightly in a pestle and mortar.

Drain the cucumber, discarding the juices. Stir in the yogurt and add the tomato, coriander and cumin. Season to taste. Cover and chill until needed.

To make the curry, make a paste by combining the grated ginger with the crushed garlic in a little bowl.

Heat the oil in the saucepan and add the cumin seeds. Stir for a few seconds to release their aroma into the oil, then add the finely chopped onions and 1 teaspoon of the ginger and garlic paste. Stir over a medium heat for 1–2 minutes until the onion begins to soften. Add the tomatoes, salt and spices, and stir well to combine. Cover the pan with a lid and cook over a gentle heat for 7–8 minutes until the tomatoes are soft and pulpy.

Whisk the natural yogurt or labneh in a medium bowl and add 6 tablespoons of the hot onion and tomato mixture, one tablespoon at a time, whisking well between each addition. Transfer the yogurt mixture back to the pan; return the pan to the heat and add the paneer (or feta) and peas. Simmer for 5 minutes, then remove the pan from the heat. Squeeze over some lime juice and taste, adding a little more if necessary. Scatter with coriander and serve with the raita and some flatbreads, or rice for a carbier option.

There are various interpretations of the Kenyan name here, including 'stretch the week' and 'feed the week' – but either way, it's delicious. You can also cook a few lamb chops or chicken thighs or drumsticks while the sakuma is simmering, and pop them on top. Scatter with lots of oregano or chopped marjoram.

Sakuma wike
tomato & kale stew

- 2 teaspoons extra virgin olive oil
- 110g onions, sliced
- 1 garlic clove, crushed
- 1 sliced red chilli (optional)
- 900g very ripe tomatoes or 500g fresh tomatoes and 1 x 400g tin of whole plum tomatoes
- 1 tablespoon chopped fresh herbs, such as thyme, flat-leaf parsley, mint, basil, lemon balm or marjoram (or a mixture)
- 250ml homemade vegetable stock or water
- 250g kale, weighed after the stalks have been removed
- 110g cooked chickpeas (optional)
- flaky sea salt, freshly ground black pepper and sugar, to taste
- chopped oregano or marjoram, to serve (optional)

Heat the olive oil in a 22cm/3.3-litre casserole over a gentle heat and sweat the onions, garlic and chilli, if using, for 5-6 minutes until soft. Cover the pan. It is vital for the success of this dish that the onions are completely soft before you add the tomatoes.

Remove the hard core from the fresh tomatoes. Put them into a deep bowl and cover with boiling water. Count to 10, then pour off the water and peel off the skins. Cut into slices, reserving the juice.

Add the fresh tomatoes (or tinned tomatoes) to the pan and season with salt, pepper and sugar. Add a generous sprinkling of chopped herbs and cook for 10–20 minutes or until the tomato softens.

Pour in 115ml vegetable stock (or water) and bring to the boil. Add the roughly chopped kale and chickpeas, if using. Return to the boil, then cook for 8–10 minutes until the kale is tender. Season to taste and sprinkle with chopped oregano or marjoram, if you wish. Serve as is, or as an accompaniment to either grilled fish or meat dishes.

Fresh jackfruit is wonderful to use here but if it's not easy to find, use a tin instead. Jackfruit has the texture of pulled pork so is a great vegan alternative to meat.

Jackfruit curry

- 2 tablespoons extra virgin olive oil
- 1 teaspoon mustard seeds
- 1 teaspoon cumin seeds
- 175g onion, diced
- 2 large garlic cloves, crushed
- 1 teaspoon freshly grated turmeric
- ½–1 teaspoon freshly grated ginger
- 1 teaspoon ground cumin
- 1 teaspoon ground coriander
- ¼ teaspoon chilli flakes
- 450g peeled and chopped ripe tomatoes or 1 x 400g tin chopped tomatoes
- 1 x 400g tin chickpeas, drained
- 1 x 560g tin jackfruit, washed and drained
- 4 tablespoons homemade vegetable stock or water
- flaky sea salt, freshly ground pepper and sugar
- lots of fresh coriander
- natural yogurt and organic lime wedges, to serve

Heat the oil in a sauté pan over a medium heat, add the mustard seeds, then as soon as they splutter, add the cumin seeds and onion, and stir-fry for 4–5 minutes or until the onion starts to soften and caramelise a little. Add the garlic, turmeric, ginger, ground cumin and coriander and chilli flakes. Continue to stir-fry for 1–2 minutes. Add the peeled and chopped tomatoes, chickpeas, jackfruit and season with salt and pepper. Bring to the boil and simmer for 10–12 minutes (you may need to add a little water if it seems a bit dry). Season with salt, pepper and sugar. Pour into a warm serving bowl. Scatter with lots of fresh coriander sprigs.

Provide a wedge of lime for each guest and offer thick natural yogurt as an accompaniment. Serve with rice or flatbreads, if you wish.

SERVES 6

Bread and butter pudding can be savoury as well
as deliciously sweet. This version makes a tasty
economical supper for six or more hungry people.
There are myriad variations here — chorizo instead of
bacon, spring onions or melted leeks with Cheddar
cheese... the choices are endless.

Gruyère, piquillo pepper & basil
bread & butter pudding

- 50g very soft butter (for buttering
  the bread and greasing the dish)
- 6 slices of good white bread
  (approx. 1–2cm thick), crusts removed –
  about 100g prepared weight
- 110g mature Gruyère cheese,
  coarsely grated
- 3 medium organic, free-range eggs
- 450ml whole milk
- 150g Piquillo peppers, diced into
  approx. 7mm cubes
- 12 basil leaves, chopped
- flaky sea salt and freshly ground
  black pepper

Grease a pie dish or ovenproof dish, approx. 24 x 17cm, with
butter, and use the remaining butter on the slices of bread.
Cut the bread into roughly 2.5cm squares and arrange in
the pie dish. It's really important to leave a generous space
between each piece of bread to allow for expansion, so the
pudding will be light and fluffy. Squash in too much bread
and the end result will be disappointingly heavy. Sprinkle the
grated cheese over the top.

Crack the eggs into a bowl and add the milk, chopped peppers
and basil. Whisk thoroughly for a minute or two, and season
well with salt and pepper.

Pour the egg and pepper mixture over the bread, and then
cover the dish with clingfilm and set aside to rest in the fridge
for a few hours for the bread to plump up, or better still
overnight, if possible.

Preheat the oven to 180°C/gas mark 4.

Bake the pudding for 40 minutes until puffed up and golden
like a soufflé.

Serve with a salad of organic leaves with a perky dressing.

You'll love this curry — even ardent curry haters can't get enough of this deliciously spiced dish. It's also an excellent base for other additions, such as chunks of cooked potato.

Vegetable & tofu curry

- 2 large garlic cloves, crushed
- 1–2 chillies, deseeded and roughly chopped
- zest of 1 organic lemon or 2 limes
- 110g coriander leaves and stalks, coarsely chopped, plus extra to serve
- 60g cashew nuts, toasted and roughly chopped
- 1½ tablespoons grated fresh ginger
- 2 teaspoons ground turmeric
- 2 teaspoons ground cumin
- 4 tablespoons extra virgin olive oil
- 1 x 400ml tin of coconut milk
- 400ml homemade vegetable stock
- 500g pumpkin or sweet potato, peeled and cut into 2cm dice
- 1 small cauliflower, weighing approx. 350g, broken into small florets
- 225g firm tofu, cut into approx. 2cm dice
- 225g French beans, green or a mixture of green and yellow
- sea salt and freshly ground black pepper
- organic lemon or lime wedges, to serve

Combine the garlic, chilli, citrus zest, roughly chopped coriander leaves and stalks, cashew nuts, ginger, turmeric, cumin and 1 teaspoon of salt in a food processor and whizz to a chunky or smooth purée, depending on your preference.

Heat the olive oil in a large saucepan over a medium heat, stir in the garlic and ginger purée and cook for 3–4 minutes, stirring. Whisk in the coconut milk and stock, bring to the boil and simmer for 8–10 minutes.

Add the chunks of sweet potato or pumpkin and return to the boil. Cover the pan with a lid and simmer for 10 minutes. Add the cauliflower florets and tofu chunks and bring back to the boil, then cover and simmer for a further 10 minutes. Add the French beans and simmer for a further 2–3 minutes, uncovered, until all of the vegetables are cooked through.

Season with salt and pepper, and squeeze over a little lemon or lime juice, to taste. Sprinkle with lots of coriander and serve with lemon or lime wedges.

RICE, GRAINS + PASTA

SERVES 6
This soup was inspired by a soup I ate and loved at the Little Fox in Ennistymon in County Clare. I'm not sure how they made it, but here is my interpretation, which I love. It's made in minutes, really sustaining and super-delicious.

Red lentil soup *with turmeric, masala yogurt, toasted seeds & coriander*

- 6 tablespoons extra virgin olive oil or butter
- 225g onions, chopped
- 2 teaspoons peeled and grated fresh turmeric
- 225g red lentils
- 1.2 litres homemade vegetable or chicken stock
- 2 teaspoons pumpkin seeds
- 2 teaspoons sunflower seeds
- 1 teaspoon each of black and white sesame seeds
- a squeeze of organic lemon juice, to taste
- flaky sea salt and freshly ground black pepper
- coriander leaves, to garnish

FOR THE MASALA YOGURT
- 1 teaspoon coriander seeds
- 1 teaspoon cumin seeds
- 6 tablespoons natural yogurt

Heat 2 tablespoons of the oil in a 22cm/3.3-litre heavy-based saucepan. Stir in the onions, then cover and sweat over a gentle heat for 5–10 minutes until soft but not coloured.

Add the fresh turmeric and cook for a minute or two before stirring in the lentils. Season generously with salt and pepper. Pour in the stock, bring back to the boil and simmer for 6–8 minutes until the lentils are soft.

Meanwhile, mix the pumpkin, sunflower and sesame seeds in a small bowl with the remaining 4 tablespoons of extra virgin olive oil.

To make the masala yogurt, combine the cumin and coriander seeds in a mortar and grind to a fine powder. Stir into the natural yogurt in a bowl and season with salt, to taste.

Whizz the soup to a coarse purée in a blender or food processor. Taste and add a squeeze of lemon juice and some more salt and pepper, if needed.

Ladle the soup into wide soup bowls, drizzle some masala yogurt over the top and sprinkle with the seeds. Garnish with fresh coriander leaves and serve as soon as possible.

SERVES 6-8

Crunchy raw cauliflower, Romanesco or calabrese are all delicious served raw in this fresh salad. However, to ring the changes you could drizzle the florets with oil and roast them on a baking tray in the oven at 200°C/gas mark 6 for 15 minutes until slightly caramelised at the edges. For a vegan version of this delicious salad, omit the labneh or yogurt — it'll still be an irresistible, nutrient-dense combination.

Cauliflower, avocado, pistachio & pomegranate freekeh

- 450g freekeh
- 6 tablespoons extra virgin olive oil, plus extra to drizzle
- 3 tablespoons white wine vinegar
- 1 teaspoon ground turmeric
- 2 teaspoons honey
- 1 small cauliflower, Romanesco or calabrese, weighing approx. 300g, divided into small florets
- 2 ripe but firm avocados, cut into chunks
- seeds from 1 small pomegranate
- 2 tablespoons nigella seeds (optional)
- 110g pistachios, coarsely chopped
- 6-8 tablespoons labneh or thick natural yogurt
- 1-2 tablespoons sumac
- flaky sea salt and freshly ground black pepper
- lots of fresh dill sprigs, to serve

Put the freekeh into a saucepan and cover with plenty of cold water. Bring to the boil and simmer for 15–45 minutes, depending on your freekeh (broken or cracked freekeh will take 15–20 minutes, whole grains will take 35–45 minutes and will absorb more water). It should be soft but still slightly chewy. Drain, season with salt, drizzle with extra virgin olive oil and toss well to coat the grains in the oil.

Meanwhile, whisk together 6 tablespoons of extra virgin olive oil, the vinegar, turmeric and honey in a small bowl. Drizzle over the warm freekeh and toss gently together.

Add the cauliflower florets, avocado and some of the pomegranate seeds (save some for sprinkling) to the freekeh, and season with salt, freshly ground black pepper and nigella seeds (if using).

To serve, pile a couple of tablespoons of the freekeh, cauliflower and avocado salad onto a plate. Sprinkle with most of the chopped pistachios and spoon a dollop of labneh or yogurt on top. Scatter a few more pomegranate seeds, some pistachio nuts, the sumac and a few sprigs of dill over the labneh or yogurt and serve immediately.

This pretty vegan salad is made with lots of edible flowers from the garden. Freekeh is a Lebanese wheat that is picked while still underripe and set on fire to remove the husk, which smokes and toasts the grain. Freekeh cooking times vary quite dramatically depending on the type and age of the freekeh, so do check the packet instructions. Add ricotta or feta here for a non-vegan variation.

Tomato salad *with flowers, za'atar* & freekeh

- 100g freekeh or farro
- 2 tablespoons pomegranate molasses or moscatel vinegar
- 5 tablespoons extra virgin olive oil, plus extra for drizzling
- 12 cherry tomatoes
- 1 ripe but firm avocado
- 1 mini Picolino cucumber
- 2 teaspoons za'atar
- lots of edible flowers, such as violas, rocket flowers, borage flowers (remove the furry calyx from behind the flower), chive or coriander blossom
- flaky sea salt and freshly ground black pepper

Put the freekeh (or farro) into a saucepan and cover with plenty of cold water. Bring to the boil and simmer for 15–45 minutes, depending on the freekeh (broken or cracked freekeh will take 15–20 minutes, whole grains will take 35–45 minutes and will absorb more water). It should be soft but still slightly chewy.

Meanwhile to make the dressing, whisk the pomegranate molasses or moscatel vinegar in a little bowl with the olive oil.

When the freekeh is cooked, drain and season well with salt and pepper. Toss with some of the dressing.

Cut the tomatoes into halves or quarters, depending on size. Peel the avocado, remove the stone and cut into 2.5cm chunks. Cut the cucumber in half lengthways, and then into thick slices at an angle.

Arrange the salad ingredients on a plate, season with salt and drizzle with a little extra virgin olive oil. Scatter with the freekeh, drizzle over the pomegranate molasses dressing and sprinkle with the za'atar and lots of edible flowers. Taste and add a few more flakes of sea salt if necessary and some freshly ground black pepper.

Polenta can be served the moment it's ready or it can
be poured into a shallow, well-oiled dish and left to
cool. It can then be sliced and chargrilled, pan-grilled,
toasted or fried and served with all sorts of toppings.
It can even be cut into thin slices and layered with a
sauce just like lasagne. The quality of polenta varies so
choose a really good brand. For a one-pot dish there are
countless possibilities for different toppings. Just use
your imagination and a little restraint.

Polenta

- 1.7 litres water
- 1 level dessertspoon salt
- 225g coarse polenta flour (bramata)
- 110g butter
- 85–110g freshly grated Parmesan
- flaky sea salt and freshly ground
  black pepper

Variations

GOAT'S CHEESE
Sprinkle the hot polenta with Gorgonzola,
Cashel Blue or goat's cheese.

POLENTA WITH ROCKET & TAPENADE
Arrange some fresh rocket leaves on the
polenta, top with tapenade (olive paste).

POLENTA WITH TOMATO
FONDUE & PESTO
Spread some hot Tomato Fondue
(page 133) on the polenta and drizzle with
a teaspoonful of your favourite pesto.

POLENTA WITH CARAMELISED
ONIONS & PESTO
Serve with some warm caramelised onions
and top with a teaspoonful of pesto.

Put the water into a deep, heavy-bottomed saucepan and
bring to the boil, add salt, then sprinkle in the polenta very
slowly letting it slip gradually through your fingers, whisking all
the time (this should take 2-3 minutes). Bring to the boil and
when it starts to 'erupt like a volcano' reduce the heat to the
absolute minimum - use a heat diffuser mat if you have one.

Cook for about 40 minutes stirring regularly.* (I use a whisk
at the beginning but as soon as the polenta comes to the boil
I change to a flat-bottomed wooden spoon.) The polenta is
cooked when it is very thick but not solid and comes away
from the sides of the pan as you stir.

As soon as the polenta is cooked, stir in the butter, freshly
grated Parmesan and lots of freshly ground pepper. Taste and
add a little more salt if necessary. It should be soft and flowing;
if it is a little too stiff, add some boiling water.

*If you stir constantly on a slightly higher heat, the cooking
time can be reduced to about 20 minutes but it is more
digestible if cooked slowly over a longer period.

Buddha bowls are delicious bowls of healthy grains, topped with fresh vegetables, fruits, herbs, seeds and protein. This is a recipe I love but feel free to change it with the seasons. If you don't have quinoa in your larder, you can use brown rice instead. Have fun designing your own Buddha bowl.

Smoked duck & quinoa *Buddha bowls*

- 225g white or red quinoa (or a mixture)
- 340ml cold water
- 2 smoked duck breasts, thinly sliced
- 2 large nectarines or peaches, thinly sliced
- 2 sweet apples, finely diced and tossed in a little organic lemon juice
- 200g cucumber or courgettes, finely diced
- 6 spring onions, sliced at an angle
- 3 tablespoons pumpkin seeds, toasted
- fresh coriander leaves, to serve

FOR THE DRESSING
- zest and juice of 2 organic limes
- 85ml extra virgin olive oil
- 2 teaspoons toasted sesame oil
- 1 tablespoon dark soy sauce
- 1 garlic clove, crushed
- 2 tablespoons chopped chives
- 2 tablespoons chopped coriander leaves
- 1 teaspoon honey

Tip the quinoa into a sieve and rinse under cold running water for 2–3 minutes. Place in a saucepan with the water and ½ teaspoon of salt. Bring to the boil, then cover and simmer over a very low heat for 10 minutes. Remove from the heat, keeping the pan covered, and set aside for a further 10 minutes.

Meanwhile, mix all of the ingredients for the dressing together in a small bowl or jar.

Toss the warm quinoa with half of the dressing and divide between 6 serving bowls.

Arrange the sliced smoked duck breasts over the quinoa. Add the sliced nectarines, apples and diced cucumber or courgette – I like to place each topping in a little pile.

Drizzle over the remaining dressing and sprinkle with the spring onions, toasted pumpkin seeds and coriander leaves.

Tuck in and enjoy.

SERVES 8

Pearl couscous is super versatile and a great base for a one-pot supper. Add roasted pumpkin or squash, toasted hazelnuts, Medjool dates, rocket, mint leaves and maybe a little pan-grilled chicken for another delicious combination.

Pearl couscous *with pomegranate, herbs, cranberries & cashew nuts*

- 4 tablespoons extra virgin olive oil
- 450g pearl couscous
- 450ml homemade chicken or vegetable stock
- 25g chopped flat-leaf parsley
- 25g chopped mint
- seeds from 1 pomegranate
- 110g spring onions (both white and green parts), chopped
- 75g toasted cashew nuts
- 50g dried cranberries
- 2 medium carrots, peeled and grated
- ½ cucumber, seeded and cut into 7mm dice
- 1 teaspoon ground cinnamon
- 1 teaspoon ground allspice
- flaky sea salt and freshly ground black pepper
- coriander and mint leaves, to serve

FOR THE DRESSING
- 50ml extra virgin olive oil
- juice of 1 organic lemon
- 1 teaspoon honey

Heat 2 tablespoons of the extra virgin olive oil in a large saucepan, add the couscous and stir for 3–4 minutes until coated and toasted. Pour in the stock, season with ½ teaspoon of salt and pepper, and bring to the boil. Cover and simmer gently, for about 10 minutes until most of the liquid has been absorbed and the couscous is al dente. Drain, toss in the remaining 2 tablespoons of extra virgin olive oil and set aside to cool.

To make the dressing, mix together the extra virgin olive oil, freshly squeezed lemon juice and honey.

Add the remaining ingredients to the cooled couscous and pour over the dressing. Mix well and season with salt and pepper. Pile into a serving dish, and scatter with the mint and coriander leaves.

This salad is delicious on its own but I love it with
roast duck. Pumpkin or butternut squash or a
mixture can be substituted for the sweet potato. Other
sweet vegetables and roast peppers can also be used.
Chickpeas or beans are another gorgeous addition.

Quinoa, sweet potato & watercress salad

- 2 large sweet potatoes, pumpkin
  or butternut squash
- 3 tablespoons extra virgin olive oil
- 1 teaspoon ground coriander
- ½ teaspoon ground cinnamon
- 4 medium onions, peeled and
  quartered
- 225g red or brown quinoa
- 350ml cold water
- 2 tablespoons toasted pumpkin seeds
- 2 tablespoons toasted sunflower seeds
- 1 tablespoon toasted sesame seeds
- 6-8 handfuls of watercress sprigs
- flaky sea salt and freshly ground
  black pepper

FOR THE ASIAN VINAIGRETTE
- juice and zest of 2 organic limes
- same volume of extra virgin olive oil
- 2 teaspoons toasted sesame oil
- 1 tablespoon soy sauce
- 1 garlic clove, crushed
- 1 chilli, finely chopped (optional)
- 5 spring onions or lots of chives,
  finely chopped
- lots of chopped basil or coriander
- 1 teaspoon granulated sugar

Preheat the oven to 230°C/gas mark 8.

Peel the sweet potato (and deseed the squash or pumpkin
if using) and cut into 1.5cm cubes. Mix the spices with the
extra virgin olive oil, toss the vegetables and spread out in an
ovenproof sauté pan. Season with salt and pepper. Roast for
20-25 minutes until golden and slightly caramelised at the
edges. Remove from the pan and set aside.

Rinse the quinoa in a sieve under cold water for 2-3 minutes
to remove the natural bitter coating. Place it in the sauté pan
with the cold water, ½ teaspoon of salt and cover with a tight-
fitting lid. Bring to the boil and then reduce the heat to very
low and cook covered for 12 minutes until the grain is tender.
Remove from the heat, leave the lid on and set aside for a
further 10 minutes.

Meanwhile, make the vinaigrette. Whisk all the ingredients
together in a bowl.

To serve, put the cooled quinoa, roast vegetables and toasted
seeds in a bowl. Drizzle with the vinaigrette, toss well. Season to
taste. Pile onto a base of watercress sprigs and serve.

SERVES 4

Rice bowls are a brilliant way to eat a riff on chirashi sushi, one of the oldest forms. I make infinite variations on the theme – slices of duck breast, rare beef, cured fish, vegetables, spring onions, pickled ginger... Just get started and this may become one of your favourite ways of eating. I love White Mausu peanut rāyu, a delicious condiment made with peanuts, sesame and chilli flakes – a fusion of Japanese and Chinese flavours.

Lazy rice bowl *with whatever you fancy* & ponzu dressing

- 225g cooked sushi rice or aged basmati rice
- 300ml cold water
- 1 avocado, sliced
- 110g smoked salmon or mackerel, diced
- 2–4 spring onions, cut at an angle
- 4 teaspoons diced pickled ginger
- 4 tablespoons pickled cucumber, cut into 2cm batons, dice or ribbons
- 4 tablespoons White Mausu peanut rāyu, if available
- 4 tablespoons chopped coriander
- 2 sheets of nori seaweed
- 1–2 tablespoons sesame seeds

FOR THE PONZU DRESSING
- 125ml dark soy sauce
- finely grated zest and juice of 2 organic lemons
- finely grated zest and juice of 2 organic oranges
- 1½ teaspoons mirin
- 1 tablespoon freshly ground black pepper
- 1 tablespoon finely chopped shallot

First prepare the sushi rice. Rinse the rice for 10 minutes in a colander or sieve under cold running water or until the water becomes clear. Tip the rice into a saucepan, cover with the water and set aside for 30–45 minutes to 'wake up the rice'.

Bring the rice to the boil and simmer for 10 minutes until all the water has been absorbed. Avoid the temptation to stir the rice or remove the lid. Increase the heat right at the end for the last 10 seconds, just before you turn off the heat. Remove the lid, place a tea towel over the rice and replace the lid. Set aside for 20 minutes.

Meanwhile, make the dressing. Whizz all the ingredients together in a blender. Season to taste.

Fill each bowl over half-full with sushi rice and top with the avocado, smoked salmon, spring onions, pickled ginger and pickled cucumber. Add a dollop of white mausu, if available. Sprinkle over some coriander, the crumbled nori seaweed and sesame seeds. Serve drizzled with the ponzu dressing.

Pearl barley is super nutritious, absolutely delicious and very versatile. I love to cook it as a pilaff and enjoy adding extra bits and pieces, depending on the season — sweet cherry tomatoes, crisp cucumber dice, roast squash or pumpkin, peas, broad beans, Romanesco or broccoli florets, spinach or kale all work well.

Pearl barley pilaff
with greens & walnuts

- 40g butter or olive oil
- 225g banana shallots, peeled and diced
- 450g pearl barley
- 1.8 litres homemade chicken stock
- 200g watercress (or rocket or sorrel), chopped
- 40g walnuts, coarsely chopped
- freshly squeezed organic lemon juice
- flaky sea salt and freshly ground black pepper

Melt the butter in a deep saucepan over a gentle heat, add the shallots and cook for 2–3 minutes until just starting to soften. Add the pearl barley and toss the grains in the butter. Season with salt and pepper. Pour in the stock and bring to the boil, then cover and simmer gently for 45 minutes–1 hour until the pearl barley is fully cooked.

You now have a platform to add lots of delicious extras: here I've added chopped watercress leaves. Stir in the chopped watercress and allow it to wilt for 2–3 minutes, then add the coarsely chopped walnuts and some freshly squeezed lemon juice. Season to taste and serve.

I can't tell you how many times this soda bread pizza base has come to the rescue when I needed to whip up a dish of something filling and delicious in no time at all. It can be as simple as a topping of grated mature Cheddar cheese or halved, well-seasoned cherry tomatoes.

Soda bread pizza
with delicious toppings

- 450g plain white flour, plus extra for kneading and rolling
- 1 level teaspoon bicarbonate of soda
- 1 level teaspoon sea salt
- 375–400ml buttermilk
- extra virgin olive oil, for brushing
- ½-1 tablespoon chopped rosemary
- 50g chorizo, sliced
- 350g Tomato Fondue (page 133) or chopped fresh or tinned tomatoes mixed with seasoning/spices
- 8 bocconcini, halved
- 15g Parmesan cheese, grated
- lots of snipped flat-leaf parsley

Fully preheat the oven to 230°C/gas mark 8.

Sift the flour, bicarbonate of soda and salt into a large bowl. Make a well in the centre. Pour in 375ml of the buttermilk and, using one hand, mix in the flour from the sides of the bowl. Mix to a softish, not too wet and sticky consistency, adding more buttermilk if necessary. When it all comes together, turn out the dough onto a floured board, knead lightly for a few seconds, tidy it up and flip it over.

Brush a roasting tin, approx. 31 x 23 x 5cm, with olive oil. Roll out the dough lightly to fit the tin and sprinkle with rosemary. Scatter the sliced chorizo evenly over the surface. Spread a layer of tomato fondue over the chorizo and arrange some halved bocconcini on top. Sprinkle over the Parmesan.

Transfer the tray to the fully preheated oven on a low rack and bake for an initial 15 minutes. Then reduce the heat to 200°C/gas mark 6 and bake for a further 20–25 minutes or until the dough is cooked and it's golden and bubbly on top.

Sprinkle with the parsley and serve with a good green salad.

Other tasty toppings

'NDUJA AND BOCCONCINI

Follow the main recipe, omitting the rosemary and replacing the chorizo with 125g 'nduja. Sprinkle with fresh marjoram to serve.

PESTO & PARMESAN

Follow the main recipe, omitting the rosemary and chorizo and replacing the tomato fondue with 3 tablespoons of loose basil or wild garlic pesto. Top with 110–150g grated mozzarella or 110–150g soft goat's cheese and 15g grated Parmesan.

TAPENADE & SOFT GOAT'S CHEESE

Follow the main recipe, omitting the rosemary and chorizo and replacing the tomato fondue with 3 tablespoons of tapenade, and the mozzarella with 110–150g blobs of soft goat's cheese.

SPICED AUBERGINE

Follow the main recipe, omitting the rosemary and chorizo and replacing with 6–8 tablespoons of Spiced Aubergine (page 118).

CHEDDAR CHEESE & SPRING ONION

Follow the main recipe, omitting the chorizo and replacing the rosemary with 4 tablespoons of sliced spring onions and the Parmesan with 100g grated mature Cheddar cheese.

SERVES 6-12

I first tasted this dish at The Bangala in Karaikudi in South India. It's one of my favourite comfort foods. Serve alone or as an accompaniment to chicken or fish. I love to sprinkle some sprigs of chervil on top – not traditional, but delicious.

Chettinad tomato rice

- 100ml extra virgin olive oil
- 100g ghee or clarified butter (page 16)
- 1 x 5cm cinnamon stick
- 4 green cardamom pods
- 2 bay leaves
- 2 onions, finely chopped
- 1–2 green chillies, halved
- 3 large ripe tomatoes, weighing approx. 300g, peeled (see page 112) and finely chopped (like a thick purée)
- 500g basmati rice, soaked for 15–30 minutes in cold water and drained
- 900ml homemade chicken stock or water
- 225ml coconut milk
- 1½ teaspoons sea salt, to taste
- ½ teaspoon ground turmeric
- chervil sprigs (optional), to serve

Heat a deep saucepan over a medium heat. Add the oil and ghee or clarified butter. Add the cinnamon, cardamom and bay leaves, followed by the onions and green chillies. Sauté for 3–4 minutes until all the ingredients turn a pale golden colour.

Add the tomatoes and stir for 3–4 minutes. Add the soaked and drained rice, chicken stock or water, coconut milk, salt and turmeric. Bring to the boil and cover with a lid. Cook over a gentle heat for about 10 minutes until the rice is cooked and all of the liquid has been absorbed. The rice will happily sit for 15–20 minutes off the heat, but I like to serve it immediately with lots of chervil sprigs on top.

What sweet agony to have to choose just one risotto for each season, when there are so many good things to embellish the already gorgeous classic. Master the basic recipe and remember the secret is to source the best-quality rice you can – carnaroli, vilano nano or a good arborio – and to have a delicious chicken, fish or vegetable broth for the base with plenty of flavour. Freshly grated Parmesan is another essential – don't forget to stir in a nice dollop of butter just before serving.

A risotto
for all seasons

FOR A CLASSIC RISOTTO
- 2 tablespoons extra virgin olive oil
- 50g butter
- 1 medium onion, finely chopped
- 400g best-quality risotto rice, such as carnaroli, arborio or vilano nano
- 1–1.3 litres hot broth or homemade chicken or vegetable stock
- 50g Parmesan cheese, freshly grated
- flaky sea salt

Melt the oil and half the butter in a 26cm heavy-based saucepan. Add the onion and sweat over a gentle heat for 5–10 minutes until soft but not coloured.

Add the rice and stir until well coated. Cook for a minute or so and then add 150ml of the broth. Continue to cook, stirring continuously, until all of the liquid has been absorbed, before adding another 150ml of broth. The heat should be brisk, but on the other hand if it's too hot the rice will be soft outside but still chewy inside. If it's too slow, the rice will be gluey. It's difficult to know which is worse, so the trick is to regulate the heat so that the rice bubbles continuously. The risotto should take about 25–30 minutes in total to cook: when it has been cooking for about 20 minutes, add the broth more gradually, only about 4 tablespoons at a time. I use a small ladle. Watch the rice very carefully from there on. The risotto is done when the rice is cooked, but still ever so slightly 'al dente'. It should be soft and creamy and quite loose, rather than thick. The moment you are happy with the texture, stir in the remaining butter and Parmesan cheese, taste and add more salt if necessary. Risotto does not benefit from hanging around – the texture should be soft and flowing.

For spring risotto, fold the chopped watercress or wild garlic into the risotto right at the end, just before you add the butter and Parmesan.

Variations

SPRING RISOTTO
WITH WATERCRESS
- 225g wild watercress sprigs, chopped or
  225g wild garlic, chopped

SUMMER RISOTTO WITH
BROAD BEANS
- 450g broad beans, blanched
- 2 handfuls of broad bean shoots
- a few broad bean flowers, if available,
  to garnish

AUTUMN RISOTTO WITH ROOTS
- 150g carrots, peeled
- 150g beetroots, peeled
- 25g butter
- ¼ teaspoon chilli flakes (optional)
- 100g chopped kale
- a few sprigs of chervil, to garnish

WINTER RISOTTO WITH
RADICCHIO OR CHICORY
- 1 head radicchio or red chicory
- 50g walnuts, coarsely chopped
- 110g blue cheese, such as Crozier Blue,
  Dolcelatte or your favourite blue
  (optional)

For summer risotto, mix in the blanched broad beans and bean shoots right at the end, just before you add the butter and Parmesan. Garnish with a few broad bean flowers, if available.

For autumn risotto, chop the peeled carrots and beetroot into 2cm dice. Sweat in 25g butter for 8–10 minutes – the length of time will depend on the age of the beets and carrot – then remove from the pan before the onion is sweated. Add the cooked carrot and beetroot to the risotto halfway through the cooking time. Add the chilli flakes when the onion is cooked (if you wish). Just before the end of cooking add the kale. Garnish with a few sprigs of chervil.

For a winter risotto, make up the risotto in the classic recipe, substituting the broth or stock with 50/50 red wine and stock (optional). Break the radicchio or chicory into small bite-sized pieces and fold in close to the end, just before you add the butter and Parmesan. Scatter over the walnuts and add a dollop of blue cheese, if you wish.

For those of you who are conditioned to cook pasta in a huge pot of boiling salted water, the idea of cooking pasta in the sauce in just one pot may be quite a stretch to consider attempting, but do try it. The starch from the pasta thickens the sauce and the pasta absorbs the flavours deliciously, it's a revelation and you'll have such fun experimenting. For some reason I still feel slightly guilty, but less washing up helps to salve my conscience. You'll need considerably more liquid than in normal pasta sauce because the pasta will absorb much of the liquid.

One-pot pasta *with tomato & chorizo*

- 2 tablespoons extra virgin olive oil
- 1 medium onion, sliced
- 1 garlic clove, crushed
- ½–1 red chilli, chopped
- 900g very ripe tomatoes, peeled (see page 112), in summer or 2½ x 400g tins of tomatoes in winter
- zest of 1 organic lemon
- 1–2 teaspoons chopped rosemary, depending on the strength of flavour
- 225g chorizo, peeled and diced
- 850ml homemade chicken or vegetable stock
- 175ml double cream
- 300–350g fettuccine or spaghetti
- 2 tablespoons chopped flat-leaf parsley
- 30g freshly grated Parmesan cheese
- flaky sea salt, freshly ground black pepper and a generous pinch of sugar, to taste

Heat the oil in a 6-litre stainless-steel saucepan. Add the onions and garlic, toss until coated, cover and sweat over a gentle heat until soft but not coloured. Add the chilli. It is vital for the success of this dish that the onions are completely soft before the tomatoes are added.

Slice the fresh or tinned tomatoes and add to the onions with all the juices and the lemon zest. Season with salt, pepper and sugar (tinned tomatoes need lots of sugar because of their high acidity). Add the rosemary. Cook, uncovered, for a further 10 minutes, or until the tomato softens. Cook fresh tomatoes for a shorter time to preserve the lively fresh flavour.

Add the chorizo, stock and cream. Bring back to the boil, add the pasta, stir gently to separate the strands and prevent sticking. Return to the boil, cover and simmer for 4 minutes and leave to sit in the tightly covered saucepan for a further 4–5 minutes, or until just al dente. When you add the dried pasta, it will seem too much but hold your nerve, it will soften within a minute or two and cook deliciously in the sauce.

Season to taste, sprinkle with lots of chopped parsley and grated Parmesan. Serve.

As you can imagine, you can vary the fish and shellfish here depending on what's freshest and best – scallops would be a super-luxurious option and even a little smoked fish is delicious.

One-pot pasta *with* shrimps, monkfish, mussels & dill

- 2 tablespoons extra virgin olive oil
- 1 medium onion, sliced
- 1 garlic clove, crushed
- ½–1 red chilli, chopped
- 900g very ripe tomatoes, peeled, in summer or 2½ x 400g tins of plum tomatoes in winter
- zest of 1 organic lemon
- 1 teaspoon roasted and coarsely ground fennel seeds
- 850ml homemade fish, chicken or vegetable stock
- 175ml double cream
- 300–350g fettuccine or spaghetti
- 450g monkfish tail, cut into 2cm dice
- 1kg mussels in their shells, washed but not debearded before cooking
- 110g peeled cooked shrimps
- 2 tablespoons chopped flat-leaf parsley
- 2 tablespoons chopped dill
- 30g finely grated Parmesan cheese
- flaky sea salt, freshly ground black pepper and a generous pinch of sugar, to taste

Heat the oil in a 6-litre stainless-steel saucepan, add the onions and garlic, and toss until coated. Cover the pan with a lid and sweat over a gentle heat until the onions are soft but not coloured. Add the chilli. It is vital that the onions are completely soft before you add the tomatoes.

Slice the fresh or tinned tomatoes and add to the pan with all the juices. Stir in the lemon zest and fennel seeds, and season to taste with salt, pepper and sugar (tinned tomatoes need lots of sugar because of their high acidity). Cook for a further 10 minutes, uncovered, or until the tomato softens. Cook fresh tomatoes for a shorter time to preserve their fresh lively flavour.

Add the stock and the cream, and bring back to the boil. Add the pasta, stirring gently to prevent it from sticking. Season again. Return the sauce to the boil, then cover and simmer for 4 minutes. Bring the sauce back the boil, and then add the monkfish and mussels. Cover the pan with a tight-fitting lid and set aside, off the heat, for a further 2–3 minutes until the monkfish turns opaque and the mussels open. Carefully stir in the cooked peeled shrimps and heat through for 1–2 minutes. Test the pasta, it should be al dente.

Season to taste, scatter with lots of chopped parsley and dill, and a sprinkling of Parmesan. Serve.

Have you ever tried cooking your spaghetti bolognaise in just one pot? It's a revelation — and much less washing up!

Spaghetti
bolognaise-ish

- 2 tablespoons extra virgin olive oil
- 115g bacon lardons
- 1 medium onion, sliced
- 1 garlic clove, crushed
- ½–1 red chilli, chopped
- 900g very ripe tomatoes, peeled, in summer or 2½ x 400g tins of plum tomatoes in winter
- 1–2 teaspoons ground cumin
- 2 tablespoons freshly chopped herbs, such as thyme, flat-leaf parsley, tarragon or rosemary (or a mixture)
- 700g organic minced beef
- 850ml homemade chicken or beef stock
- 300–350g spaghetti
- 2 tablespoons chopped flat-leaf parsley
- 30g finely grated Parmesan
- flaky sea salt, freshly ground black pepper and a generous pinch of sugar, to taste

Heat the oil in a 6-litre stainless steel saucepan and add the bacon lardons. Stir and cook for 3–4 minutes before adding the onions and garlic. Toss until well coated. Cover the pan with a lid and sweat over a gentle heat until the onion is soft but not coloured. Add the chilli. It is vital for the success of this dish that the onions are completely soft before the tomatoes are added.

Slice the fresh or tinned tomatoes and add to the pan with all the juices. Season with salt, pepper and sugar (tinned tomatoes need lots of sugar because of their high acidity). Stir in the cumin and fresh herbs. Bring to the boil, then reduce the heat and simmer, uncovered, for just 10 minutes until the tomatoes soften. Cook fresh tomatoes for a shorter time to preserve their fresh lively flavour.

Crumble in the well-seasoned minced beef, stir and cook for 3–4 minutes. Pour in the stock and return to the boil, then add the spaghetti, stirring gently to separate the strands. Return the sauce to the boil, then cover the pan with a lid and simmer for 4–5 minutes or until the pasta is al dente.

Season to taste, scatter with lots of chopped parsley and Parmesan. Serve.

Try this fun way to cook pasta – all in one pot.
Sounds like sacrilege, but it works brilliantly.

One-pot *mushroom* pasta

- 30g butter
- 85g onion, finely chopped
- 225g flat mushrooms, sliced
- a squeeze of organic lemon juice
- 3 tablespoons chopped flat-leaf parsley
- 1 teaspoon thyme leaves
- ½ tablespoon chopped chives
- 2 tablespoons chopped marjoram
- 900ml homemade vegetable or
  chicken stock
- 125ml double cream
- 300–400g fettuccine or spaghetti
- 30g freshly grated Parmesan cheese
- flaky sea salt and freshly ground
  black pepper

Melt the butter in a 25cm/3.2-litre casserole until it foams. Stir in the onion, cover with a lid and sweat over a gentle heat for 5–10 minutes until soft but not coloured. Remove the onion to a bowl.

Cook the sliced mushrooms in the hot casserole, in batches if necessary. Season each batch with salt, pepper and a tiny squeeze of lemon juice. Add the onion back to the pan, together with 1 tablespoon of parsley and the thyme. Pour in the stock and cream, bring to the boil and simmer for 3–4 minutes. Season to taste.

Add the pasta, stirring to separate the strands and prevent it from sticking, and boil for 4 minutes. Then turn off the heat and allow the pasta to stand, tightly covered with a lid, for 4–5 minutes or until it is al dente.

Sprinkle with the remaining parsley and the grated Parmesan. Taste and add a little more lemon juice, if necessary. Serve.

SWEET THINGS

Clafoutis is a sort of fluffy custard, a base for whatever seasonal fruit you can lay your hands on: rhubarb or gooseberries are delicious, but you need to adjust the sugar. This one is made with stone-in damsons or you can use Mirabelle plums. I often have rose geranium or mint sugar in a jar – this also makes a delicious sprinkle.

Damson clafoutis

- 15g softened butter, for greasing
- 5 organic, free-range eggs
- 100g caster sugar
- 75g plain white flour
- 115ml double cream
- 420ml whole milk
- ½ teaspoon ground cinnamon or ½ teaspoon pure vanilla extract
- 750g damsons or Mirabelle plums or cherries, peaches, nectarines or greengages, in season
- 25g pistachio nuts, coarsely chopped or flaked almonds
- icing or caster sugar, to sprinkle
- softly whipped cream, to serve

Preheat the oven to 180°C/gas mark 4 and grease a 28cm round baking dish or similar with softened butter.

Whisk the eggs with the caster sugar in a mixing bowl. Sift in the flour, pour in the cream and milk, and add the cinnamon or vanilla extract. Whisk together to form a smooth batter with no lumps.

Pour half the batter into the buttered dish. Scatter the damsons or Mirabelle plums on top. (I leave the stones in, but you could de-stone them if you wish. If using cherries or greengages, you can scatter them over whole, or stone them if you prefer; peaches or nectarines are best halved or quartered, depending on size.) Pour the remaining batter over the fruit.

Bake for 30–40 minutes, and then scatter with the pistachios or flaked almonds and continue to cook for a further 10 minutes until the clafoutis is puffed up and the nuts are golden. Sprinkle with icing or caster sugar, to serve. Accompany with lots of softly whipped cream.

Many pears need a little help from aromatic herbs or spices to enhance their flavour. This recipe for poached pears infused in basil syrup is a wonderful dessert — and I've also included lots of variations for you to try once you've mastered the basic method.

Poached pears *with basil syrup*

- 200g granulated sugar
- 450ml water
- 6–8 basil leaves
- 45ml freshly squeezed organic lemon juice
- 4 firm pears, such as Conference, Doyenne du Comice or Bartlett

Variations

POACHED PEARS WITH SAFFRON SYRUP

Replace the basil with 6 lightly crushed whole cardamom pods and ¼ teaspoon of good-quality saffron threads.

LEMON POACHED PEARS

Replace the basil with the thinly pared rind and juice of 1 organic lemon.

SWEET GERANIUM POACHED PEARS

Replace the basil with 3–4 large sweet geranium leaves (*Pelargonium graveolens*).

LEMON VERBENA POACHED PEARS

Replace the basil with 4–6 lemon verbena leaves.

GINGER POACHED PEARS

Replace the basil with a 2.5cm piece of fresh ginger, cut into thin slivers.

Put the sugar, water, basil and lemon juice into 32.5cm stainless-steel sauté pan and stir over a gentle heat to dissolve the sugar. Bring to a simmer.

Meanwhile, start on the pears. Peel, halve and core the pears, leaving the stalks intact, and as you finish each one pop it into the simmering syrup, cut-side up. Cover the surface of the pan with a paper lid to prevent the cut surface from discolouring, then pop on the lid of the pan, and cook gently for 20–30 minutes, spooning the syrup over the pears every now and then.

Carefully remove the pears and arrange them in a serving dish in a single layer, cut-side down. Taste the syrup and, if necessary, simmer over a gentle heat with the lid off for a few minutes to concentrate the flavour. Be careful not to cook it for too long, or the syrup will caramelise.

Remove the basil and pour the syrup over the pears then set aside to cool. Serve chilled.

The poached pears will keep for several weeks, covered, in the fridge.

SERVES 10-12

This is definitely my 'go-to' recipe for a super quick and delicious comfort pud. Even though I call this version with plums Autumn Tart, I make it throughout the year with different fruits, including rhubarb, gooseberries, greengages, peaches, nectarines, apples and pears, and add a few juicy fresh berries when I have them. The sponge base is quick to make in a food processor and you can ring the changes by experimenting with different flavours, such as freshly chopped lemon verbena, rose geranium or rosemary.

Autumn tart

FOR THE FRUIT BASE
- 175g granulated sugar
- 110ml water
- 450g plums, halved and stoned,
  or dessert apples, such as Egremont
  Russet, Cox's Orange Pippin or
  Charles Ross, peeled and cut into
  quarters or eighths, depending on size

FOR THE SPONGE TOPPING
- 150g softened butter
- 150g granulated sugar
- 200g self-raising flour
- 3 organic, free-range eggs

Preheat the oven to 160°C/gas mark 3.

Put the sugar and water into a 25cm ovenproof sauté pan or cast-iron frying pan and stir over a medium heat until the sugar has dissolved. Continue to cook, without stirring, until the sugar caramelises to a rich golden brown (if the caramel is not dark enough, the tart will be too sweet).

Once the caramel darkens to a golden brown, remove the pan from the heat and arrange the prepared fruit, cut-side down, in a single layer over the caramel.

To make the sponge topping, combine the butter, sugar and flour in the bowl of a food processor. Whizz for a second or two, then add the eggs and stop as soon as the mixture comes together. Spoon the cake mixture over the plums and spread gently to create an even layer.

Bake for about 1 hour. The centre should be firm to the touch and the edges slightly shrunk from the sides of the pan.

Remove from the oven and set aside to rest in the pan for 4–5 minutes before turning out. Serve with crème fraîche or softly whipped cream.

Variations

ROAST APPLES WITH CINNAMON SUGAR
Add 1 teaspoon of ground cinnamon to the granulated sugar.

ROAST APPLES WITH SULTANAS & HAZELNUTS
Add 1 scant teaspoon of sultanas and 1 teaspoon of coarsely chopped toasted hazelnuts to the granulated sugar for each apple. Top each apple with a tiny blob of butter.

SERVES 9

Don't forget this simple recipe for a much-loved autumn or winter dessert — a great way to use up any last windfall cooking apples. I love to roast them in an enamel roasting tin. For a special dish, you could vary the fillings and allow your guests to select their favourite. Soft brown sugar and cream is a compulsory accompaniment. Nowadays, baked apples are often stuffed with 'exciting' mixtures which may include dried fruit, lemon rind, nuts and spices. This is nice occasionally, but my favourite is still the simple roast apple of my childhood. It's important to note that the apples will cook much faster in the autumn than they will later on in the year, when they will have most probably come from a cold store.

A tray of roast apples

- 9 large cooking apples,
  preferably Crimson Bramley
- 9 tablespoons granulated sugar
- 25g butter
- 150ml water
- softly whipped cream and
  soft dark brown sugar, to serve

MARZIPAN ROAST APPLES

Fill the apple cavities with
225g marzipan mixed with
½ teaspoon of ground cinnamon.

**ROAST APPLES WITH
PEDRO XIMENEZ RAISINS**

Soak 110g raisins in warm Pedro Ximenez sherry for at least 30 minutes, or better still overnight. Combine the raisins with 4 tablespoons of caster sugar and use to fill the apples. Top with butter and bake as above. Serve with 225ml softly whipped cream mixed with 3 tablespoons of Pedro Ximenez.

Preheat the oven to 180°C/gas mark 4.

Core the apples and score the skin of each around the 'equator'. Arrange the apples in a single layer in an ovenproof dish large enough to take the apples in a single layer, approx. 31 x 25 x 5cm, and for the simplest but nonetheless totally delicious version, fill the centre of each one with 1 generous tablespoon sugar. Put a little dab of butter on top of each.

Pour a little water around the apples and roast in the oven for about 1 hour. They should be fluffy and burst slightly when they are fully cooked, but still be fat and puffy (not totally collapsed). Serve as soon as possible with softly whipped cream and soft brown sugar.

Roasting a stone fruit is a simple, easy way to rustle up a delicious dessert. I like to vary the fresh herbs and flavourings from season to season, to include lemon thyme, marjoram or lemon verbena, which all add a bit of magic. This version is extra gorgeous with homemade vanilla or honey and lavender ice cream.

Roast peaches, nectarines or apricots *with honey & lavender*

- 8 peaches, nectarines or apricots, halved and stoned
- 2 tablespoons honey
- 2 tablespoons freshly squeezed organic lemon juice
- 25g butter
- 1–2 teaspoons dried lavender buds

TO SERVE
- a few fresh lavender flowers (if available)
- softly whipped cream or crème fraîche

Preheat the oven to 250°C/gas mark 9.

Arrange the prepared fruit, cut-side down, in a single layer in an ovenproof dish approx. 31 x 25 x 5cm and drizzle with the honey. Squeeze over the lemon juice and put a little dab of butter on each piece of fruit. Sprinkle with the dried lavender and roast for 8–10 minutes.

Serve warm, sprinkled with a few lavender flowers (if available) and accompanied by homemade vanilla or honey and lavender ice cream, or softly whipped cream or crème fraîche.

French toast is so good that you can almost forget how economical it is. It is a brilliant way to use up leftover bread or brioche that might otherwise be wasted. Every country has its own version of this simple dish. I've eaten variations from India to the UK, where it's also called knights of Windsor, or poor knights or eggy bread. Then there's German toast, known as gypsy toast, torrija in Spain, Bombay toast and, of course, the French classic pain perdu. It's actually better if the bread is a little stale. You may want to add a little vanilla extract to the batter when serving a sweet version and a dash of cream. Make individual toasts or cover the whole base of the pan with a pain perdu for sharing.

Pain perdu

- 3 organic, free-range eggs
- 175ml whole milk
- a tiny pinch of salt
- 6 slices of white bread or brioche
- 4 tablespoons butter (clarified butter, page 16 is best)
- fresh berries and icing sugar, to serve

Whisk the eggs, milk and salt together in a bowl until well blended. Strain the mixture into a shallow bowl in which you can easily soak the bread. Dip both sides of each slice of bread or brioche in the batter.

Melt 2 tablespoons of the butter in a frying pan. Fry the bread over a medium heat until very lightly browned, turning once. Repeat with the remaining bread and butter. Serve warm with fresh berries and a generous sprinkling of icing sugar.

Tasty toppings

Serve with sliced and sugared strawberries, raspberries and/or blueberries, mascarpone and lots of shredded mint.

Serve with a blob of sweet apple sauce and a dusting of ground cinnamon.

Serve with sliced banana, a blob of chilled natural yogurt, some roughly chopped walnuts and maple syrup.

Variations

SPICED FRENCH TOAST
Add ½ teaspoon of ground cinnamon or nutmeg to the batter.

FOR CITRUS FRENCH TOAST
Add 2 teaspoons of grated organic lemon or orange zest to the batter.

A dish of roasted fruit couldn't be simpler – rhubarb, plums, greengages, apricots, peaches, apples or pears. I love to add some freshly chopped herbs, such as rose geranium or lemon verbena to the sugar or the accompanying cream. I've become a huge fan of the sweet and intense flavour of roast rhubarb.

Roast rhubarb

- 1kg red rhubarb
- 200–250g granulated sugar
- 2-3 teaspoons freshly chopped herbs, such as rose geranium or lemon verbena (optional)
- ice cream, labneh or thick Jersey cream, to serve

Trim the rhubarb stalks if necessary. Slice the rhubarb into 2.5cm pieces and arrange in a single layer in a 45 x 30cm non-reactive ovenproof dish. Scatter the sugar over the rhubarb and leave to macerate for 1 hour or more, until the juices start to run.

Preheat the oven to 200°C/gas mark 6.

Cover the rhubarb with a sheet of parchment paper and roast in the oven for 10–20 minutes, depending on the thickness of the stalks, until the rhubarb is just tender. Keep a close eye on the rhubarb as it can disintegrate very quickly

Serve hot or cold with ice cream, labneh or thick Jersey cream.

SERVES 6

This is a superb recipe – a one-pot compote with an intense flavour – which keeps brilliantly in a fridge for a week or more.

Myrtle's compote of pears

- 6 ripe pears
- 110g granulated sugar
- 1 organic lemon

Halve the pears, peel thinly and core carefully, keeping a good shape. Put them in a pan which will just fit them nicely. Add the sugar, a few thin strips of lemon rind and the lemon juice. Cover with a well-fitting lid and cook gently for 20–30 minutes until soft. Cool and serve alone or with softly whipped cream.

SERVES 10-12

You'll find yourself reaching for this recipe over and over again. Here I use apple and blackberries with sweet geranium, but I also love it with green gooseberries and elderflower, or plums. I enjoy arranging the blackberries and apples in neat lines, but if you are super busy just sprinkle them over the top of the sponge base.

Apple & blackberry traybake
with sweet geranium sugar

- 8–12 lemon geranium leaves
  (*Pelargonium graveolens*)
- 3–4 cooking apples, such as
  Bramley Seedling or Grenadier
- 150g blackberries
- 75g caster sugar
- crème fraîche or softly whipped
  cream, to serve

FOR THE SPONGE BASE
- 225g softened butter
- 175g caster sugar
- 275g self-raising flour
- 4 organic, free-range eggs

Preheat the oven to 160°C/gas mark 3.

Line the base of a 33 x 23 x 5cm cake tin, or a 25.5cm sauté pan or cast-iron frying pan with parchment paper, allowing it to hang over the sides. Arrange 6–8 sweet geranium leaves over the base – these give the sponge a haunting lemony flavour.

To make the sponge base, combine the butter, sugar and flour in the bowl of a food processor. Whizz for a second or two, then add the eggs and stop as soon as the mixture comes together. Spoon the mixture over the base of the tin as evenly as possible (over the sweet geranium leaves).

Peel the apples. Cut into thin slices and arrange on top of the sponge in three lines. Arrange a line of blackberries in between each row. Sprinkle 25g of the caster sugar over the top and bake for about 50 minutes.

Meanwhile, whizz 2–4 sweet geranium leaves with the remaining 50g caster sugar in a food processor. Spread over a baking tray and set aside at room temperature to dry out.

Once it is fully cooked, the centre of the cake should be firm to the touch and the edges slightly shrunk from the sides of the tin. Serve in the tin, sprinkled with the sweet geranium sugar. Alternatively, leave to rest in the tin for 4–5 minutes before turning out. Serve with crème fraîche or softly whipped cream.

These are made in minutes and are pretty irresistible. If you want to ring the changes, try one of the equally delicious variations listed below. The dry ingredients may be weighed up ahead – even the day before. You can rub in the butter in advance, but do not add the raising agent and liquid until just before cooking.

Sticky orange swirls

- 75g cold butter, plus extra for greasing
- 450g plain white flour
- a pinch of salt
- 1½ teaspoons baking powder
- 25g caster sugar
- zest of 1 organic orange
- 2 small organic, free-range eggs
- 200ml whole milk
- egg wash, made by beating
  1 small organic, free-range egg with
  1 dessertspoon milk
- 25g demerara sugar

FOR THE ORANGE BUTTER

- 75g softened butter
- 1½ teaspoons finely grated organic
  orange zest
- 100g icing sugar

Preheat the oven to 250°C/gas mark 9 and grease a 33 x 23 x 5cm cake tin, with a little butter.

First make the orange butter. Cream the butter with the orange zest. Add the icing sugar and beat until fluffy. Set aside.

Sift the flour into a large wide bowl, add a pinch of salt, the baking powder and the caster sugar. Finely grate the zest of the orange into the bowl. Mix the dry ingredients together with your hands, to incorporate as much as air as possible.

Cut the cold butter into cubes or grate coarsely and toss well in the flour. Using the tips of your fingers, rub in the butter until the mixture resembles large flakes. Make a well in the centre. Whisk the eggs with the milk in a jug and pour all at once into the well. Using the fingers of your 'best hand' outstretched and stiff, combine the ingredients in a full circular movement from the centre to the outside of the bowl.

Sprinkle some flour on your work surface and turn out the dough. Tidy around the edges of the dough, then flip it over and roll or pat it gently into a 30 x 20cm rectangle about 2cm thick.

Slather most of the soft orange butter evenly over the dough, then roll it up tightly from the long side. Divide into four quarters, and then cut each piece into three to give you 12 pieces altogether. Brush the cut side of each swirl with the egg wash and dip in the demerara sugar. Arrange side by side in the buttered roasting tin, leaving a little room for expansion. Bake for 10 minutes.

Serve while still warm, or at room temperature, with a little extra orange butter. Pull apart gently like a tear and share.

This dessert can be made ahead and enjoyed warm or cold. Rosewater varies in strength so be careful to add gradually and taste.

Kheer marwadi
Indian rice pudding

Variations

CHOCOLATE & HAZELNUT SWIRLS

Make the dough and roll out into a rectangle about 2cm thick. Slather with 6-8 tablespoons of chocolate and hazelnut spread, then roll up lengthways like a Swiss roll and cut into 12 pieces. Brush the cut side of each swirl with egg wash and sprinkle with coarsely chopped toasted hazelnuts. Bake for 10–12 minutes.

MARMALADE SCONES

Make the dough as before and roll out into a 2cm-thick rectangle. Slather with 6-8 tablespoons of marmalade (chop the peel finely first), then roll up lengthways like a Swiss roll and cut into 12 pieces. Brush the cut side of each swirl with egg wash and bake for 10–12 minutes.

CINNAMON
BUTTER SCONES

Make the dough and roll out into a 2cm-thick rectangle. To make the cinnamon butter, cream together 150g softened butter, 250g pale brown sugar and 1 tablespoon of ground cinnamon. Slather the cinnamon butter over the dough, roll up lengthways like a Swiss roll and cut into 12 pieces. Brush the cut side of each swirl with egg wash. Mix 25g granulated or demerara sugar with 1 teaspoon of ground cinnamon and sprinkle over the surface. Bake for 10 minutes.

- 1 tablespoon coconut oil
- 50g basmati rice, soaked for an hour in cold water and drained
- 1 litre coconut milk
- 500ml water
- 3 tablespoons whole almonds, skinned and chopped very finely or ground to a paste
- 100g granulated sugar
- 50g fresh coconut, grated
- 25g raisins
- 50g pistachio nuts, cut into slivers
- 50g blanched almonds, cut into slivers
- ½ teaspoon ground seeds from green cardamom pods
- 2 teaspoons kewra essence or rosewater, to taste
- chopped pistachios and rose petals, to serve

Heat the coconut oil in a pan. Add the soaked and drained rice and stir for 2–3 minutes. Pour in the coconut milk and water, and simmer over a low heat for 1 hour until the rice has absorbed all of the liquid and the pudding has thickened.

Stir in the almonds, sugar, coconut, raisins, pistachios and almond slivers. Cook for a couple of minutes, stirring, until the sugar has dissolved. Remove the pan from the heat and stir in the ground cardamom and kewra or rosewater. Set aside to cool, and then chill until ready to eat.

To serve, spoon into individual dishes and sprinkle with the chopped pistachios and rose petals, if available.

We make this simple pudding regularly in the summer – loganberries, tayberries and boysenberries also work brilliantly, as do blackberries during the wild blackberry season.

Raspberry tatin

- 50g butter
- 75g caster sugar
- 350g raspberries
- 2 tablespoons chopped sweet geranium leaves (*Pelargonium graveolens*)
- 125g grated Bramley Seedling apples
- softly whipped cream or crème fraîche, to serve

FOR THE CAKE
- 150g butter
- 150g caster sugar
- 3 large organic, free-range eggs
- 150g self-raising flour
- 25g ground almonds
- zest of 1 organic lemon
- 5–6 sweet geranium leaves (*Pelargonium graveolens*)

Preheat the oven to 180°C/gas mark 4.

Heat the butter and sugar in a 25cm ovenproof sauté pan over a low heat, stirring until melted. Simmer for 3–4 minutes, stirring frequently. Spread over the bottom of the pan and arrange the raspberries in a single layer over the top. Sprinkle with the chopped sweet geranium leaves and the grated Bramley apple.

Cream the butter and sugar until pale and creamy. Beat in the eggs, one at a time. Sift in the flour and fold into the batter. Fold in the ground almonds and lemon zest, or put everything into a food processor and whizz for 30 seconds–1 minute, just enough to combine.

Spoon the mixture over the fruit, lay 5 or 6 geranium leaves over the surface and bake for 50 minutes. If it's browning too quickly, cover with an enamel plate or lay a piece of baking parchment on top. Leave to cool for 10 minutes, then turn out onto a serving plate and remove the geranium leaves if you wish.

Serve with softly whipped cream or crème fraîche.

Chocolate puddings run neck and neck with apple tarts as people's favourite dessert. My version is wickedly rich with a melting texture. It should be moist and gooey in the centre, so don't overcook it or it will be disappointing and dull. This one is surprisingly good served cold.

Chocolate fudge pudding *with* toasted hazelnuts & Frangelico cream

- 150g unsalted butter, plus extra for greasing
- 150g good-quality chocolate (I use 52% cocoa solids)
- 1 teaspoon vanilla extract
- 150ml warm water
- 100g caster sugar
- 4 organic, free-range eggs
- 25g self-raising flour

TO SERVE
- icing sugar, to dust
- 225ml softly whipped cream or crème fraîche mixed with 1 tablespoon Frangelico hazelnut liqueur
- a few toasted hazelnuts, coarsely chopped

Preheat the oven to 200°C/gas mark 6 and grease a 1.2-litre pie dish with a little butter.

Chop the chocolate into small pieces and melt with the butter in a Pyrex bowl set over a pan of hot, but not simmering, water. As soon as the chocolate has melted, remove the bowl from the heat and add the vanilla extract. Stir in the warm water and sugar and mix until smooth.

Separate the eggs and whisk the yolks into the chocolate mixture. Then fold in the sifted flour, making sure there are no lumps.

In a separate bowl, whisk the egg whites until stiff peaks form, and then gently fold them into the chocolate mixture. Pour the chocolate mixture into the buttered dish.

Put the dish in a bain-marie and pour in enough boiling water to come halfway up the sides of the dish. Bake for 10 minutes. Then reduce the temperature to 160°C/gas mark 3 for a further 15–20 minutes or until the pudding is firm on top, but still soft and fudgy underneath and saucy at the base.

Set aside to cool slightly before dusting with icing sugar. Serve warm or cold sprinkled with toasted hazelnuts with Frangelico cream or crème fraîche alongside.

This is my original bread and butter pudding recipe, the one that people tell me over and over again is the best they've ever tasted. But there's nothing frugal about this recipe – it's got lots of plump dried fruit in it and a generous proportion of cream to milk. When people taste it, they say 'Wow!' I know it has a lot of cream in it, but don't skimp – just don't eat it every day! I play around with this formula and continue to come up with more and more delicious combinations, depending on what's in season and what I have to hand (see below for some of my favourite additions). It may come as a surprise, but this bread and butter pudding reheats perfectly.

Bread & butter pudding

- 50g softened butter, preferably unsalted, plus extra for greasing
- 12 slices good-quality white bread, crusts removed
- ½ teaspoon freshly grated nutmeg or ground cinnamon or mixed spice
- 200g plump raisins or sultanas
- 450ml double cream
- 225ml whole milk
- 4 large organic, free-range eggs, lightly beaten
- 1 teaspoon vanilla extract
- 110g granulated sugar, plus 1 tablespoon for sprinkling
- a pinch of salt
- softly whipped cream, to serve

Grease a 25 x 20.5cm rectangular ovenproof dish with butter, then butter the bread. Arrange 4 slices of bread, buttered-side down, in one layer in the base of the buttered dish. It's really important to leave a generous space between each slice of bread to allow for expansion, so the pudding will be light and fluffy. Squash in too much bread and the end result will be disappointingly heavy.

Sprinkle the bread with half the freshly grated nutmeg (or cinnamon or mixed spice) and half the raisins or sultanas. Arrange another layer of bread on top, buttered-side down, and sprinkle with the remaining spice and dried fruit. Cover with the remaining bread, buttered-side down. Leave the slices whole or cut into quarters.

In a bowl, whisk together the cream, milk, eggs, vanilla extract, sugar and a pinch of salt. Pour the mixture through a fine sieve over the bread. Sprinkle 1 tablespoon of sugar over the top and set aside, loosely covered, at room temperature for at least 1 hour or cover and chill overnight.

Preheat the oven to 180°C/gas mark 4.

Put the dish in a bain-marie, and pour in enough boiling water to come halfway up the sides of the baking dish. Bake in the middle of the oven for about 1 hour or until the top is crisp and golden. Serve the pudding warm, with lots of softly whipped cream.

Variations

BARMBRACK BREAD & BUTTER PUDDING

Replace the bread with barmbrack and use mixed spice or cinnamon in place of the nutmeg.

PANETTONE BREAD & BUTTER PUDDING

Replace the bread with panettone.

HOT CROSS BUN BREAD & BUTTER PUDDING

Replace the bread with sliced hot cross buns.

MARMALADE BREAD & BUTTER PUDDING

Slather the buttered bread generously with Seville orange marmalade. You could also serve some marmalade sauce as an accompaniment or, for an extra treat, flavour the softly whipped cream with Cointreau.

CROISSANT & CHOCOLATE BREAD & BUTTER PUDDING

Use 4 (leftover or stale) croissants instead of bread. Replace the spices and raisins with 1 tablespoon of chocolate chips.

Coffee crème brûlée

- 4 large or 5 small organic, free-range egg yolks
- 40g caster sugar
- 1½ tablespoons Camp coffee essence
- 200ml whole milk
- 200ml double cream
- 8 teaspoons demerara sugar

Preheat the oven to 150°C/gas mark 2.

Whisk the egg yolks with the caster sugar in a mixing bowl until well combined. Add the coffee and whisk again. Pour in the milk and cream and whisk gently to combine.

Pour the mixture through a nylon sieve into a 19cm round ovenproof dish, approx. 4.5cm deep. Put the dish in a bain-marie, and pour in enough boiling water to come halfway up the side of the dish. Bake for 45–50 minutes until just set, but still slightly wobbly in the centre.

Sprinkle lightly with demerara sugar: it should be a thin layer, so tip off any excess if necessary. Glaze with a blowtorch.

Coffee crème brulée is already very rich, but you could serve it with a little pouring cream, if you wish, and some nougatine biscuits or ladyfingers.

Make a whole dish of Tiramisu to delight your friends. The name means pick-me-up, which is not surprising considering the amount of booze it contains. Tiramisu originated in Venice, but is now served in Italian restaurants all over the world – and it always seems to taste different. I've had rave reviews for this version, which is very easy to assemble.

Tiramisu

- 450ml strong espresso coffee
- 3 tablespoons brandy
- 3 tablespoons Jamaican rum
- 75g dark chocolate (I use 60% cocoa solids Valrhona)
- 3 organic, free-range eggs, separated
- 3 tablespoons caster sugar
- 255g mascarpone
- 38–40 ladyfinger or boudoir biscuits
- unsweetened cocoa powder, to dust

Mix the coffee with the brandy and rum. Roughly grate the chocolate (I do it in the food processor with the pulse button). Whisk the egg yolks with the sugar until the mixture reaches the 'ribbon' stage and is light and fluffy, then fold in the mascarpone one tablespoon at a time.

In a separate bowl, whisk the egg whites until stiff peaks form. Fold gently into the mascarpone mixture.

Now you are ready to assemble the tiramisu. Dip each side of the biscuits, one at a time, into the coffee mixture and arrange side by side in a 25.5 x 20.5cm dish with low sides, or a parchment-lined 20.5 x 10cm loaf tin. Spread half of the mascarpone mixture gently over the biscuits and sprinkle half of the grated chocolate on top. Arrange another layer of soaked biscuits over the grated chocolate and spoon over the remaining mascarpone. Cover the dish with clingfilm and set aside in the fridge for 3–4 hours, or preferably overnight, to allow the sponge biscuits to soak up all the delicious flavours.

Just before serving, scatter the remaining chocolate over the top and dust with unsweetened cocoa powder.

If you used a loaf tin, unmould the tiramisu before serving and sprinkle with a little extra grated chocolate. Serve in thick slices with lots of whipped cream – decadent and delicious.

Tiramisu will keep for several days in the fridge, but make sure it is covered so that it doesn't pick up other flavours.

Variation
FROSTED TIRAMISU

Freeze the Tiramisu in a parchment-lined 20.5 x 10cm loaf tin. Serve in thick slices with Irish coffee sauce. To make the sauce, put 175g granulated sugar and 75ml water in a heavy-bottomed saucepan; stir until the sugar dissolves and the water comes to the boil. Remove the spoon and do not stir again until the syrup turns a pale golden caramel. Then add 225ml coffee and return to the heat to dissolve to a liquid once again. Leave to cool and then stir in 1 tablespoon of Irish whiskey.

This is a super versatile recipe that comes from Sue Cullinane, one of our senior tutors at Ballymaloe Cookery School. I sometimes just scatter crunchy praline over the top for a quick, but delicious fix. Toasted hazelnuts are also a delectable combination, instead of the walnuts.

Sue's coffee & walnut cake

- 225g softened butter, plus extra
  for greasing
- 100g caster sugar
- 80g soft brown sugar
- 300g self-raising flour
- 2 teaspoons baking powder
- 4 organic, free-range eggs
- 2 tablespoons whole milk
- 1 tablespoon Camp coffee essence

FOR THE COFFEE BUTTERCREAM
- 100g softened butter
- 300g icing sugar, sifted
- 1 dessertspoon whole milk
- 2 teaspoons Camp coffee essence
- 20 walnut halves, to decorate

Preheat the oven to 180°C/gas mark 4. Grease a 25.5. x 18cm Swiss roll tin with a little butter and line with a sheet of parchment paper that comes up over each side.

Put all the cake ingredients into a food processor. Whizz just long enough to combine. Spread the cake mixture evenly over the lined tin and smooth the top with a palette knife. Bake for 20–25 minutes until well risen. Remove from the oven and set aside to cool completely in the tin.

To make the buttercream, cream the butter and beat in the icing sugar, followed by the milk and coffee extract.

As soon as the cake has cooled, use a palette knife to spread the coffee buttercream evenly over the top. Cut into squares and decorate each one with a half walnut. Alternatively, pipe a rosette of coffee buttercream on top of each square and top with a toasted nut.

This makes a delicious nibble to enjoy with a
shot of espresso to round off a meal.

Chocolate bark *with many good things*

- 150g chocolate (approx. 62% cocoa solids)
- 25g toasted hazelnuts, coarsely chopped
- 25g toasted almonds, coarsely chopped
- 25g pistachios, halved
- 50g sour cherries or dried cranberries, halved, or plump raisins or candied orange peel or a mixture (dried white mulberries are another delicious option)

Line a baking tray with baking parchment.

Break the chocolate into a Pyrex bowl and sit over a saucepan of cold water. Make sure the water does not touch the bottom of the bowl. Turn on the heat under the saucepan and bring the water to the boil. Turn off the heat immediately and allow the chocolate to melt gently in the residual heat.

Pour out the chocolate onto the lined baking tray and spread out to a thickness of 5mm (approx. 20cm square). Don't worry if the edges are not even – it doesn't matter.

Sprinkle the nuts and fruit evenly over the chocolate and leave to set. Cut into rectangles or break into uneven chunks.

Serve with coffee.

Index

Acknowledgements

My 19th book and I still can't type, how feeble is that…? In fact, I should say it's OUR 19th book because Rosalie Dunne who was my PA for 24 years has typed my challenging scrawl for each and every one – so a huge thank you, yet again, to dear Rosalie – you are a total star.

My tutors here at Ballymaloe Cookery School: Tracie, Pat, Gary, Richard, Sorcha, Pam, Florrie, Shermin and Tiffin tested and re-tested recipes with me and I mustn't forget Tim and our farm garden team, Haulie, Eileen, Igor, David who grow the most beautiful produce for us year round – that's what makes my simple pared-back food sing.

My current PA, Sharon Hogan, supports me in a myriad of ways to meet the deadlines.

My patient editor, Vicky Orchard, cajoles and encourages and doles out huge dollops of sage advice. Special thanks to you and to Lizzie Mayson for the beautiful photos, and of course thank you Annie Rigg for cooking my food and making it look so beautiful on the page.

Finally, to Tim and all our children and grandchildren, I love when we all sit down around the kitchen table to enjoy a bubbling pot of deliciousness together. This is what memories are made of…